Ben Fullbrook was called to the Bar in 2016 and practises planning and public law at Landmark Chambers, which is ranked by the Legal 500 as the leading UK set for planning law. He has represented clients at a range of planning inquiries and in the High Court and Court of Appeal.

An introduction to the General Permitted Development Order

An introduction to the General Permitted Development Order

Ben Fullbrook
Barrister, Landmark Chambers

Law Brief Publishing

Published 2021 by Law Brief Publishing, an imprint of Law Brief Publishing Ltd
30 The Parks
Minehead
Somerset
TA24 8BT

www.lawbriefpublishing.com

Paperback: 978-1-913715-33-5

To Bex, Elly, Josh and Zach

PREFACE

It seems likely that the GPDO will play a part in the government's plan to expand house building and transform town centres over the next few years, just as it has played its part in helping businesses mitigate some of the effects of COVID-19 "lockdown". Now therefore seems to be an appropriate time for an introductory work to help improve understanding of the topic, particularly among those not already well-versed in the planning system.

The opportunity to write a book on planning law is, quite frankly, not one which I deserve and it is certainly not one for which I would have been equipped were it not for my membership of Landmark Chambers. Since their inexplicable decision to take me on as a pupil and then as a tenant I have received an inordinate amount of advice and encouragement from my colleagues. Space does not allow me to name them all, but I would like to mention in particular: Richard Turney (who I have badgered perhaps more than most), Zack Simons (who is also the author of the excellent Planoraks blog), Guy Williams (who, as my pupil supervisor, first introduced me to planning law), Galina Ward (who is a constant source of wise counsel) and Matthew Henderson (who also has to put up with me as a roommate). Particular thanks must also go to my excellent clerks Richard Bolton and Ana Martins for their patience and understanding. I am also very grateful to the team at Law Brief Publishing whose idea this book was and who have provided me with a great deal of support along the way.

Above all others, though, thanks must go to my wife Bex, who has had to put up with me writing (and talking about) this book whilst also parenting three children (now aged 1, 3 and 4) through about 12 months of near isolation. The Bible says that a wife of noble character is worth far more than rubies (Prov 31:10) and, whilst I hope she does not take that too literally, my debt to her is surpassed only by that which I owe to the subject of that ancient book – who has shown me love beyond measure.

The law stated in this book is correct as of 2 April 2021.

Ben Fullbrook
April 2021

CONTENTS

CHAPTER ONE

INTRODUCTION

The purpose of this book

1. The rights contained within the Town and Country Planning (General Permitted Development) Order 2015 "the GPDO" have been expanded in recent years and this is set to continue as the government sets out to fulfil its ambition of deregulating the planning system and increasing housebuilding. It is likely that most property owners have relied on the GPDO, knowingly or unknowingly, at some point.

2. This book is aimed at lay people and legal practitioners alike. It is not intended to be an exhaustive treatise on the GPDO or a legal commentary. Instead, it focuses on a number of key, overarching practical principles and a selection of those permitted development rights which are either most frequently used in practice or most likely to be used by people without ready recourse to legal expertise.

What is the GPDO and what does it do?

3. Perhaps the most basic rule of planning law is that no *"development"* of land can take place without planning permission.[1] The term *"development"* is very broadly defined as *"the carrying out of building, engineering, mining or other operations in, on, over or under land, or the making of any material change in the use of any buildings or other land."*[2] Examples of activities which have been found to amount to *"development"* include the hammering of 554 marker stakes into a

---

[1] Town and Country Planning Act 1990, s.57(1)

[2] TCPA 1990, s.55(1)

field[3] and the change in use of a building from a single dwellinghouse to a *"house let in lodgings"*.[4]

4. It is important to note that the statutory definition of *"development"* contains within it some specific exceptions. These include the following, which do not amount to *"development"*:[5]

   a. The carrying out for the maintenance, improvement or alteration of any building of works which affect only the interior of the building, or do not materially affect the external appearance of the building;

   b. The use of any buildings or other land within the curtilage of a dwellinghouse for any purpose incidental to the enjoyment of the dwellinghouse as such;[6]

   c. The use of any land for the purposes of agriculture or forestry;

   d. Changes of use which are specified in an order made by the Secretary of State;[7]

5. Planning permission is therefore not required for any of the above. However, even with these exceptions, it remains the case that planning permission is required for a wide range of fairly ordinary activities, such as erecting a garden shed, laying a driveway and hanging a sign outside a shop. If local planning authorities[8] were

---

[3] *Beronstone Ltd v First Secretary* [2006] EWHC 2391 (Admin)

[4] *Birmingham Corporation v Minister of Housing and Local Government* [1964] 1 QB 178

[5] TCPA 1990, s.55(2)

[6] For more detail on the meaning of the terms *"curtilage"* and *"dwellinghouse"* see paragraphs 61–67 below. As to the meaning of *"incidental to"* see paragraph 90 below.

[7] Principally, those changes of use covered by the Town and Country Planning Use Classes Order 1987

[8] Typically district, borough and unitary authorities, see TCPA 1990, s.1

required to process applications for all of these types of development they would quickly be overwhelmed. As a consequence, Parliament has provided the Secretary of State with the power to make development orders, which have the effect of deeming a grant of planning permission for certain, specified development.[9] The principal such order, and the subject of this book, is the GPDO.[10]

The scope of permitted development rights

6. The GPDO applies to all land in England.[11] Article 3(1) grants planning permission for the development listed in sch. 2 of the Order (subject to a number of exceptions and restrictions – see below). Schedule 2 is currently divided into 21 parts and each part is sub-divided into various classes of development. These are as follows:

    a. Part 1 *"Development within the curtilage of a dwellinghouse"*. This includes rights relating to the extension and alteration of dwellinghouses (Classes A-D)[12], the erection of ancillary buildings (Class E) and hard surfacing (Class F);

    b. Part 2 *"Minor operations"*. This includes the erection of gates, fences and walls (Class A), the creation of access to a highway (Class B) and exterior painting (Class C);

    c. Part 3 *"Changes of use"*. This includes changes of use from restaurants/cafes/takeaways to retail (Class A) and vice versa (Class C), shops to financial and professional (Classes D & F) and vice versa (Class E), offices and

---

[9] TCPA 1990, s.59(3)

[10] It should be noted that local planning authorities also have the power to make Local Development orders pursuant to the TCPA 1990, s.61; however these are not covered by this book

[11] GPDO, art.1(2)

[12] Although this does not extend to rebuilding: ***Sainty v Minister of Housing and Local Government*** (1964) 15 P. & C.R. 432

storage to dwellinghouses (Classes O & P), agricultural buildings to dwellinghouses (Class Q)

d. Part 4 *"Temporary buildings and uses"*. This permits the erection of certain temporary structures and temporary uses, such as markets.

e. Part 5 *"Caravan sites and recreational campsites"*. This permits the use of land in certain circumstances for campsites and other purposes.

f. Part 6 *"Agricultural and forestry"*. This permits certain development, for example the erection of structures on agricultural and forestry land.

g. Part 7 *"Non-domestic extensions, alterations, etc"*. This permits certain development relating to shops, offices, warehouses, schools and hospitals.

h. Part 8 *"Transport related development"*. This permits certain development relating to railways, ports, airports and waterways. The rights are only available to specified undertakers, not the public at large.

i. Part 9 *"Development relating to roads"*. This permits various highway works carried out by highways authorities and undertakers. It also permits works required for the maintenance of unadopted streets or private ways.

j. Part 10 *"Repairs to services"*. This permits the carrying out of any works for the purposes of inspecting, repairing or renewing any sewer, main, pipe, cable or other apparatus, including breaking open any land for that purpose.

k. Part 11 *"Heritage and demolition"*. This permits certain works to be undertaken for the preservation of *"any building or monument"*. The development must be carried out by or on behalf of Historic England. It also contains rights relating to the demolition of buildings and certain means of enclosure.

l. Part 12 *"Development by local authorities"*. This permits local authorities to, among other things, erect certain structures, including bus shelters, drinking fountains, bins and horse troughs.

m. Part 12A *"Development by local authorities and health service bodies"*. This is an emergency measure brought in for the purpose of responding to the Covid-19 pandemic.

n. Part 13 *"Water and sewerage"*. This provides a range of rights to statutory undertakers, drainage bodies and the Environment Agency relating to watercourses and sewerage.

o. Part 14 *"Renewable energy"*. This includes installation of solar equipment, ground source heat pumps and installation or alteration of wind turbines.

p. Part 15 *"Power related development"*. This permits certain development relating to gas and electricity supply.

q. Part 16 *"Communications"*. This permits, among other things, the installation, alteration and maintenance of various pieces of communications infrastructure. It also covers the installation of post boxes.

r. Part 17 *"Extensions, alterations etc ancillary to mining operations"*. This allows for a range of development relating to mining operations, including certain operations necessary for maintenance or safety.

s. Part 18 *"Miscellaneous development"*. This permits development authorised by local or private acts of parliament and other orders, and the erection of certain structures at amusement parks.

t. Part 19 *"General development by the Crown"*. This permits a range of development undertaken by or on behalf of the Crown or on Crown land.

u. Part 20 *"Construction of new dwellinghouses"*. This permits the replacement of certain buildings with dwellinghouses and the addition of dwellings to other buildings.

7. It is worth noting that, as well as being used to actually carry out development, the rights contained within the GPDO are frequently used by developers as so-called *"fall-back positions"* to support applications for planning permissions. In essence, developers seek to persuade planning authorities to grant planning permission for a particular development by inviting a comparison between it and development which they could undertake without planning permission. Planning authorities are obliged to have regard to the existence of *"fall-back positions"* when determining planning applications, provided there is a likelihood or *"real prospect"* of those positions being realised if planning permission is refused.[13] It has been said that *"for a prospect to be a real prospect it does not have to be probably or likely: a possibility will suffice"*.[14] Whether there is a *"possibility"* will be a fact specific judgment which will need to be made by the decision maker in each case. Thus, it does not always follow that an applicant will need to specify precisely how he would make use of any permitted development rights available to him.[15]

---

[13] ***R v Secretary of State for the Environment Ex p Ahern*** [1998] Env. L.R. 189, p.9

[14] ***Mansell v Tonbridge & Malling BC*** [2017] EWCA Civ 1314, §27

[15] Ibid.

CHAPTER TWO

GENERAL PRINCIPLES

Interpretation

8. Article 2(1) GPDO contains a list of definitions. This list is not exhaustive and a number of terms are separately (and sometimes differently) defined in the part of the schedule in which they appear. Where the GPDO gives no definition of a particular word, it is worth consulting the TCPA 1990[16] as the definitions contained therein will apply to the GPDO absent any contrary intention.[17]

9. Where no relevant definition can be found, the Court of Appeal has explained that:

> *The correct approach to construing provisions of the GPDO was aptly described by Neil Cameron QC sitting as a deputy judge of the Queen's Bench Division in Evans v Secretary of State for Communities and Local Government [2015] JPL 589, para 17: "The ordinary meaning of the language used is to be ascertained when construing the development order in a broad or common sense manner." To put it as did Vincent Fraser QC sitting as a deputy judge of the Queen's Bench Division in Waltham Forest London Borough Council v Secretary of State for Communities and Local Government [2013] EWHC 2816 (Admin) at [17], "one would expect common words to be given their common meaning unless there was something which clearly indicated to the contrary". So...one must begin with a straightforward interpretation of [the word] in that provision, giving it its natural and ordinary meaning; and then consider whether there is anything in the*

[16] Particularly s.336

[17] Interpretation Act 1978, s.11

> *legislative context to displace that meaning. This should not be an unduly complicated exercise.*[18]

10. In reality, however, because the GPDO creates rigid rules which are intended to apply to a wide range of circumstances, the scope and effect of the Order can give rise to planning disputes.

11. Article 2(2) GPDO provides important guidance on measuring height (which is integral to a number of the rights contained in sch.2). It states:

> *Unless the context otherwise requires, any reference in this Order to the height of a building or of plant or machinery is to be construed as a reference to its height when measured from ground level; and for the purposes of this paragraph "ground level" means the level of the surface of the ground immediately adjacent to the building or plant or machinery in question or, where the level of the surface of the ground on which it is situated or is to be situated is not uniform, the level of the highest part of the surface of the ground adjacent to it.*

When the GPDO will not apply

12. Given the broad range of rights conferred by the GPDO it will come as no surprise to learn that the Order contains a number of provisions restricting or modifying its application in certain circumstances, principally in order to protect sites and assets that are particularly sensitive to development. These are as follows.

Development affecting European Sites or European Offshore marine sites

13. Article 3(1) GPDO makes any grant of planning permission under the Order subject to regs.75-78 of the Conservation of Species and

---

[18] ***R (Mawbey) v Lewisham BC*** [2019] EWCA Civ 1016, Lindblom LJ at §20

Habitats Regulations 2017 ("the Habitats Regs"). Regulation 75 states:

> *5. General development orders*
>
> *It is a condition of any planning permission granted by a general development order made on or after 30th November 2017, that development which—*
>
> *(a) is likely to have a significant effect on a European site or a European offshore marine site (either alone or in combination with other plans or projects), and*
>
> *(b) is not directly connected with or necessary to the management of the site,*
>
> *must not be begun until the developer has received written notification of the approval of the local planning authority under regulation 77 (approval of local planning authority).*

14. The term *"European site"* is defined in reg.8 of the Habitats Regs. The term *"European offshore marine site"* is defined in reg.18 of the Offshore Marine Conservation Regulations.[19] Guidance for determining whether a particular site will be affected has been produced by the Department for the Environment Food and Rural Affairs and Natural England.[20]

15. It is important to note that these provisions do not prevent the GPDO applying to development which meets the criteria in reg.75. Rather, it is a condition of any planning permission granted under the GDPO that development must not begin until the developer has received written notification of the approval of the local planning authority under reg.77 of the Habitats Regs.

[19] See reg. 3(1) of the Habitats Regs

[20] https://www.gov.uk/guidance/protected-sites-and-areas-how-to-review-planning-applications#check-if-a-protected-site-is-affected

Where Permitted Development rights have been removed by virtue of a condition attached to an existing planning permission

16. Section 72 of the TCPA 1990 provides local planning authorities with the power to grant planning permission subject to conditions. It is possible for conditions to be imposed which restrict or prevent reliance on certain permitted development rights. Article 3(4) GPDO clarifies that, where such a condition has been imposed, it will not be superseded by the Order.

17. Any person faced with such a condition will need to be certain of its effect. This will depend on the precise wording of the condition. The starting point for the correct approach to the interpretation of planning conditions is set out in the Supreme Court's decision in ***Trump International v Scottish Ministers*** [2015] UKSC 74. In ***Dunnett Investments Ltd v Secretary of State*** [2017] EWCA Civ 192, Hickinbottom LJ held:

    In relation to the interpretation of, specifically, a planning condition which is said to exclude the operation of the GPDO, other authorities are of some assistance. From them, the following themes can be discerned:

    - *It is rightly common ground that a planning condition on a planning consent can exclude the application of the GPDO (see Dunoon Developments v Secretary of State for the Environment and Poole BC (1993) 65 P. & C.R. 101; [1992] J.P.L. 936 ("Dunoon Developments")).*

    - *Exclusion may be express or implied. However, because a grant of planning permission for a stated use is a grant of permission for only that use, a grant for a particular use cannot in itself exclude the application of the GPDO. To do that, something more is required (see, e.g. Dunoon Developments at [107] per Sir Donald Nicholls VC).*

- *In Carpet Decor (Guilford) Ltd v Secretary of State for the Environment (1981) 261 E.G. 56, Sir Douglas Frank QC sitting as a Deputy High Court Judge said that, because in the absence of such a condition the GPDO has effect by operation of law, the condition should be in "unequivocal terms". Although "unequivocal" was used by Mr Katkowski in his written argument, during the course of debate he accepted that that term was now less appropriate, given the modem trend away from myopic focus upon the words without proper reference to their full context. However, he submitted (and I accept) that, to exclude the application of the GPDO, the words used in the relevant condition, taken in their full context, must clearly evince an intention on the part of the local planning authority to make such an exclusion.*[21]

18. By way of illustration, in ***Dunnett***, the Court of Appeal held that a planning condition which stated that the property could be used for *"no other purpose whatsoever, without express planning consent from the Local Planning Authority first being obtained"*, was held to exclude the operation of the GPDO.

19. It is also worth noting that the GPDO itself imposes conditions excluding permitted development rights in some cases.[22]

Where the existing building or use is unlawful

20. Article 3(5) of the GPDO provides that any planning permission granted under the Order will not apply if:

---

[21] Para. 37

[22] See, for example, GPDO, sch.2, pt.1, para.AA1(a)

(a) in the case of permission granted in connection with an existing building, the building operations involved in the construction of that building are unlawful;

(b) in the case of permission granted in connection with an existing use, that use is unlawful.

21. It will be recalled that *"development"* (i.e. operational development or material changes of use) requires planning permission. Therefore development will only be lawful if such permission has been obtained (expressly or via a development order such as the GPDO) or it is immune from enforcement action.[23] Broadly speaking, operational development and any material change of use of a building to use as a single dwellinghouse will be immune from enforcement action after 4 years; any other breach of planning control (e.g. any other material change or breach of a condition) will be immune from enforcement action after 10 years.[24]

22. It should be noted that art.3(5) will continue to apply even after a developer has obtained prior approval to exercise a permitted development right (see below). For example, where a developer obtains prior approval for a particular development, but then undertakes separate unlawful development before commencing the development for which he has obtained prior approval, the subsequent development may be unlawful.[25]

23. The definition of *"building"* in the GPDO[26] includes *"part of a building"*. Therefore, if any part of a building is unlawful, a developer will not be able to avail himself of the rights contained within the GPDO.[27] This will still be the case even where the right in question

---

[23] TCPA 1990, s.191(2).

[24] TCPA 1990, s.171B

[25] ***RSBS Developments Ltd v SSHCLG*** [2020] EWHC 3077 (Admin)

[26] GPDO, art.2(1)

[27] This was confirmed by Neil Cameron QC (sitting as a Deputy High Court Judge) in ***Evans v SSCLG*** [2015] EWHC 4111 (Admin),

is for a change of use so long as the change of use sought is in connection with a building.[28]

Where the land is controlled by a section 106 agreement

24. It is not uncommon for developers seeking planning permission to enter into planning obligations with the planning authority, requiring them to undertake certain activities on the land or to contribute certain sums to support other local amenities. These are often referred to as s.106 agreements and can contain terms which have the effect of preventing certain types of development which would otherwise be possible under the GPDO. Such agreements cannot supersede or amend the GPDO and so a breach of the agreement would not result in planning enforcement action. It would, however, amount to a breach of covenant and could be restrained by an injunction or a claim for damages.

Where the land is subject to restrictive covenants

25. Both freehold and leasehold titles can be subject to restrictive covenants which run with the land and which prohibit certain forms of development and activities. These covenants are not always enforceable, for example, if they have been waived or if they were not properly registered. However, that is a private law matter and beyond the scope of this book. Where these covenants are valid, a developer will be in the same position as he would be if a s.106 agreement were in place (as described above).

Where an article 4 direction is in place

26. Article 4 of the GPDO provides local planning authorities and the Secretary of the State with the power to make a direction restricting the availability of some or all of the permitted development rights contained in the GPDO in specified areas or in relation to specified

---

[28] ***RSBS Developments Ltd v SSHCLG*** [2020] EWHC 3077 (Admin)

development. Certain types of permitted development are excluded from article 4 directions. These are as follows:[29]

a. Development permitted by any class in schedule 2 which is expressed to be subject to prior approval where, in relation to that development, the prior approval date occurs before the date on which the direction comes into force and the development is completed within a period of 3 years starting with the prior approval date;

b. Development permitted by class B of part 9 of schedule 2;

c. Development mentioned in class A of part 16 of schedule 2, unless the direction specifically so provides;

d. Development permitted by class A of part 18 of schedule 2 authorised by an Act passed after 1st July 1948 or by an order requiring the approval of both Houses of Parliament approved after that date;

e. Development permitted by class Q, R, S or T of part 19 of schedule 2;

f. Development permitted under schedule 2 in an emergency.

27. Article 4 directions must be made in accordance with a certain procedure, which is specified in sch. 3 GPDO.

28. The Planning Practice Guidance ("PPG"), published by the Ministry for Housing, Communities and Local Government ("MHCLG")

[29] GPDO, art. 4(2)

gives guidance about when article 4 directions should generally be used:[30]

> *When is it appropriate to use article 4 directions?*
>
> *The use of article 4 directions to remove national permitted development rights should be limited to situations where this is necessary to protect local amenity or the wellbeing of the area. The potential harm that the direction is intended to address will need to be clearly identified, and there will need to be a particularly strong justification for the withdrawal of permitted development rights relating to:*
>
> - *a wide area (eg those covering the entire area of a local planning authority, National Park or Area of Outstanding National Beauty)*
> - *agriculture and forestry development. Article 4 directions related to agriculture and forestry will need to demonstrate that permitted development rights pose a serious threat to areas or landscapes of exceptional beauty*
> - *cases where prior approval powers are available to control permitted development*
> - *leisure plots and uses*
> - *the installation of microgeneration equipment*

29. Article 4 directions should be construed in accordance with the same principles used for interpreting planning permissions as set out in

[30] PPG, para. 038 Reference ID: 13-038-20190722, https://www.gov.uk/guidance/when-is-permission-required

Trump International v Scottish Ministers [2015] UKSC 74.[31] Where a developer disputes the interpretation of an article 4 direction he must bring an appeal to the planning inspectorate. Any attempt to resolve the matter by issuing a claim in the courts for a declaration (under Part 8 of the Civil Procedure Rules) will be an abuse of process.[32]

30. It should be noted that an article 4 direction does not prevent <u>any</u> development of the type specified; developers are still entitled to seek planning permission from their local planning authority in the usual way.

Development requiring Environmental Impact Assessment

31. Article 3(10) GPDO provides that development which is deemed to be *"EIA development"* is not permitted under the GPDO. *"EIA development"* is defined in reg. 2 of the Town and Country Planning (Environmental Impact Assessment) Regulations 2017 ("the EIA Regs").

32. In practice this means that any development falling within the descriptions contained in sch. 1 of the EIA Regs[33] will not benefit from permitted development rights. Any development falling within sch. 2 of the EIA Regs[34] may benefit from permitted development rights, but only if the local planning authority has adopted a screening opinion (or the Secretary of State has made a screening direction) confirming that the development will not have significant

---

[31] ***R (Berkshire Assets (West London) Ltd) b Hounslow LBC*** [2018] EWHC 2896 (Admin), para. 46

[32] ***T & P Real Estate Ltd v Sutton LBC*** [2020] EWHC 879 (Ch)

[33] These include, for example, certain nuclear power stations, certain airports and certain waste disposal installations: EIA Regs, sch.1, para. 1

[34] These include certain agriculture, mining, and urban development projects that meet specified indicative thresholds

effects on the environment by virtue of factors such as its nature, size or location.[35]

Land falling within a Conservation Area, AONB, National Park or World Heritage Site

33. Certain areas are exempted from GPDO rights or subject to modified rights, as specified in sch.2 GPDO. These areas are listed in art.2(3) and sch.1, para. 1 and are referred to throughout the GPDO as "article 2(3) land". Listed buildings are also sometimes specified as being subject to modified rights.

Conditions, limitations and exceptions

34. Article 3(2) GPDO states that any permission granted under the Order is *"subject to any relevant exception, limitation or condition specified in Schedule 2."* The distinction between *"exceptions"*, *"limitations"* and *"conditions"* is a subtle but important one.

35. A limitation[36] is broadly understood to define the scope of the permitted development. This is usually set out in the first line of each particular class in sch.2: for example, pt.1, para.A1 *"the enlargement, improvement or other alteration of a dwellinghouse"*. The enlargement, improvement or other alteration of a building which is not a dwellinghouse will exceed this limitation and will be beyond the scope of this particular right.

36. Many rights also contain express exceptions, which state that the development described will not be permitted in certain circumstances. Thus, sch.2, pt.1, para.A2 states *"In the case of a dwellinghouse on article 2(3) land, development is not permitted by Class A if—(a) it would consist of or include the cladding of any part of the exterior of the dwellinghouse with stone, artificial stone, pebble dash,*

---

[35] Article 3(10) of the GPDO is subject to several exceptions specified in art. 3(12)

[36] This is not to be confused with the case law on limitations arising from the description of development on a planning permission, as to which see the line of authorities following ***I'm Your Man Ltd v SSfE*** (1999) 7 P.&C.R.251.

render, timber, plastic or tiles... ". An exception can be treated as being largely equivalent to a limitation since this too will define the scope of the development. If development is undertaken which exceeds a limitation or exception in any respect then the whole of the development will lose the benefit of planning permission under the GPDO. This is relevant for enforcement purposes because it means that an enforcement notice would have to be directed at the whole development.

37. The position is different for conditions, which are expressly identified for each class of rights in sch. 2. A breach of a condition is a different type of breach of planning control[37] and does not infect the whole development. As a consequence an enforcement notice can be limited to the breach of the condition only.

Prior approval

38. One common condition imposed by the GPDO is a requirement to obtain prior approval of certain aspects of the proposed development from the local planning authority.[38] Recent expansions of the GPDO have tended to include requirements for prior approval on a widening range of issues. Some confusion exists about the nature of prior approval applications and the factors which a planning authority is entitled to take into account when determining them.

The nature of prior approval applications

39. It is important to stress that a prior approval application is not an application for planning permission; nor does the grant of prior approval confer any planning permission – this is already conferred by virtue of art.3(1) GPDO, as explained above. Thus, even where prior approval has been granted, this is not a guarantee that the

---

[37] TCPA 1990, s.171A

[38] See, for example, GPDO, sch. 2, pt. 1, para. A4(2)

development falls within the scope of the relevant permitted development right.[39]

40. Prior approval applications are better understood as conditions precedent to commencing development. It is extremely important that developers comply precisely with the relevant prior approval requirements and do so before commencing development. If they do not, the development will not be permitted development and will be unlawful.[40] The only option for a developer in such a situation would be to apply for retrospective planning permission.[41]

41. Prior approval may be granted subject to conditions.[42]

The form of prior approval applications

42. There is no prescribed form for a prior approval application. Indeed in ***Murrell v SSCLG*** [2010] EWCA Civ 1367, Richards LJ described the process of applying for a determination as to whether prior approval is required as being:

> *attended by the minimum of formalities and ... simple to operate. The application for determination as to whether prior approval is required does not need to be in any particular form and does not need to be accompanied by anything more than a written description of the proposed development and of the materials to be used and a plan indicating the site, together with the required fee... When an application is submitted, it engages a two-stage process ... The first stage involves consideration of whether prior approval is required. If the council determines that it is not required, it should notify the applicant accordingly. If it determines that prior approval is*

---

[39] ***Keenan v Woking BC*** [2017] EWCA Civ 438

[40] For an example of this, see ***Maximus Networks Ltd v SSCLG*** [2018] EWHC 1933 (Admin)

[41] See ***Winters v SSCLG*** [2017] EWHC 357 (Admin), paras. 19 and 23

[42] ***Pressland v Hammersmith and Fulham LBC*** [2016] EWHC 1763 (Admin)

> *required and notifies the applicant of the decision, it moves into the second stage, in which it has ... to decide whether to give approval.*[43]

Time limits

43. Once a prior approval application has been submitted, a local planning authority must determine it within the period specified in the relevant provision of sch.2 or, if no period is specified, within a period of eight weeks beginning with the day immediately following that on which the application is received by the authority.[44] An extension to these time periods may be *"agreed between the applicant and the authority in writing"*.[45] The Court of Appeal has confirmed (in a majority judgment) that this will include an oral agreement that can be evidenced in writing – and the court advised parties to promptly record in writing any such agreements which they reach.[46] However, it is not sufficient for the applicant and authority to agree a general extension of time; it must be possible to identify the longer period.[47]

44. If no determination has been made before the specified or agreed time period has expired then the applicant will be deemed to have fulfilled the relevant prior-approval condition. This does not mean, however, that the application will automatically be permitted development, where it otherwise falls outside the scope of the relevant right (by for example exceeding a limitation or exception).[48]

45. Nevertheless, as a consequence or the above, it may be of significant importance for local planning authorities and applicants to be able

---

[43] Para. 29

[44] GPDO, art. 7

[45] ***Gluck v SSHCLG*** [2020] EWHC Civ 1756

[46] Ibid., para.

[47] Ibid., paras. 36-7 & 40

[48] See ***Keenan v Woking BC*** [2017] EWCA Civ 438

to evidence the date and time on which the application was received. It is also important to note that, where a fee is required, an application will only be complete once the fee has been paid.[49]

The factors which a local planning authority can take into account when determining a prior approval application

Whether the proposed development falls within the scope of the relevant permitted development right

46. It previously appeared to be the case that planning authorities, when determining applications for prior approval under the GPDO, were only empowered to consider the matters relevant to whether prior approval was required (i.e. those factors specifically listed in the relevant prior approval condition) and not whether the development proposed otherwise fell within the definitional scope of the particular class of permitted development relied on. The principal authority for this proposition was thought to be the judgment of Lindblom LJ (with whom Lewison LJ agreed) in ***Keenan v Woking Borough Council*** [2017] EWCA Civ 438.

47. In ***Keenan***, the claimant applied to the defendant local planning authority for prior approval for the construction of a hardcore track. The defendant failed to respond within the specified 28 days and the claimant constructed the track. The defendant issued an enforcement notice in respect of the track. The claimant appealed the enforcement notice and contended *inter alia* that the track did not constitute a breach of planning control because it was permitted development under the predecessor to Class A by virtue of the defendant's failure to respond to the prior approval application within the specified 28 days.

48. Indeed, in ***R. (Marshall) v East Dorset DC*** [2018] EWHC 226 (Admin), Lang J held (§41, emphasis added):

---

[49] ***Infocus Public Networks v SSCLG*** [2010] EWHC 3309 (Admin), para. 11

> *"It was confirmed in **Keenan**, at [35], that the 'prior approval' conditions do not even come into play unless the proposed development falls "squarely within the description of "permitted development", in the relevant class". However, **Keenan** also decided that the local planning authority, when deciding a prior approval application under the terms of the GPDO, is not empowered, either expressly or implicitly, to decide whether or not the proposed development comes within the description of the relevant class in the GPDO: see per Lindblom LJ at [36] – [38].*

49. However, the position was recently revisited by the Court of Appeal in ***Westminster City Council v Secretary of State of Housing, Communities and Local Government*** [2019] EWCA Civ 2250.[50] Giving judgment, Hickinbottom LJ (with whom Lewison and Asplin LJJ agreed) sought to clarify the position in ***Keenan***, noting in particular that the argument being addressed in that case was whether a planning authority's failure to determine an application for prior approval would effectively deem a grant of planning permission even where the proposed development did not otherwise qualify as permitted development. That was materially different from the argument arising in ***Westminster***. At §49(i), he stated (emphasis added):

> *In **Keenan** (at [36]), Lindblom LJ said that an application to a local planning authority for a determination as to whether its "prior approval" would be required does not impose on the authority a duty to decide whether the proposed development is in fact permitted development under the GPDO. But the thrust of that paragraph of Lindblom LJ's judgment was that, by requiring a developer to seek prior approval limited to restricted planning issues, that did not confer upon the authority a power to grant planning permission for development outside the defined class of permitted development. On an application to an authority for a*

[50] Also known as ***New World Payphones***

determination as to whether its "prior approval" is required, then the authority is bound to consider and determine whether the development otherwise falls within the definitional scope of the particular class of permitted development.

50. Of course, where a planning authority is concerned that a development has been or will be undertaken which goes beyond the scope of the permitted development right relied upon, it will be entitled to take enforcement action. This will be so regardless of whether the development has been granted prior approval.

The NPPF and the local development plan

51. Certain prior approval conditions in the GPDO expressly require planning authorities to have regard to the National Planning Policy Framework ("NPPF") *"so far as relevant to the subject matter of the prior approval, as if the application were a planning application"*[51] – in other words they must treat the NPPF as a material consideration, which is not binding but should be followed absent good reason to the contrary. It is a little unclear what the words *"as if the application were a planning application"* are intended to achieve because (as explained) prior approval applications are most definitely not planning applications and different considerations apply.

52. Unlike with applications for planning permission, local planning authorities are not under any statutory duty to have regard to, and determine applications in accordance with, the local development plan. However, where relevant, development plan policies may still be material considerations.[52]

---

[51] For example, sch. 2, pt.3, para. W(10)

[52] See ***J C Decaux v FSS*** [2003] EWHC 407 (Admin) for a decision which confirms this principle in the analogous field of advertisement control.

Consultation

53. Depending on the terms of the particular permitted development right relied upon, the local planning authority may be required to carry out a consultation as part of the prior approval process – both with local occupiers and, where necessary, with specified statutory consultees.[53]

Other information

54. In addition, a local planning authority is under a duty to take reasonable steps to acquaint itself with the relevant information to enable it to make its decision correctly.[54] Thus, where, for example, a prior-approval condition requires it to assess the noise impacts of the development[55] a planning authority may judge it necessary to obtain an expert assessment of these impacts. The GPDO allows local planning authorities to request developers to submit *"such information as the authority may reasonably require in order to determine the application"*.[56] It may be necessary to agree an extension of time for this purpose. If the applicant does not agree one or respond promptly then then he runs the risk of his application being refused.

Challenging a prior approval decision

55. The means by which a prior approval decision can be challenged depend on whether it has been granted or refused.

---

[53] See, in particular sch.2, pt.3, para.W(5)-(8). For an example of a failure to conduct a lawful consultation under the GPDO see ***R (Coventry Gliding Club) v Harborough DC*** [2020] EWHC 3059 (Admin).

[54] ***Secretary of State for Education v Tameside MBC*** [1977] AC 1014 at 1065

[55] For example, sch.2, pt.3, class C

[56] For example, sch. 2, pt.3, para. W(9)

56. Where an application has been refused, a developer may appeal to the Secretary of State.[57] The time limit for bringing an appeal is six months. The appeal will typically be determined by a planning inspector, appointed by the Secretary of State and will constitute a full re-consideration of the application. Appeals will usually be dealt with by way of written representations, but may be dealt with by way of oral hearings or, in rare cases, inquiries.

57. Where an application for prior approval has been granted then there is no right of appeal for third parties. Their only option would be to bring a judicial review of the planning authority's decision. Judicial review claims are heard by the High Court and claimants must show that the planning authority has committed some legal error which vitiates its decision. Such claims must be brought within a strict time limit. In the case of prior approval decisions, this is 6 weeks from the date of the grant.[58]

58. If a judicial review succeeds, the court will usually quash (or set aside) the grant of prior approval. It is generally understood that where a grant is quashed it is treated as if it never had any legal effect.[59] Typically the planning authority would then go on to reconsider the matter applying the correct legal principles. However, some planning authorities and developers have argued that this is not possible and that, instead, the developer must be treated as having complied with the relevant prior approval condition. This is because the effect of the quashing and the passage of time (successful judicial reviews typically take several months to resolve) mean that the relevant deadline for determining the prior approval application will have expired by the time judgment is handed down (see "time limits" above). This issue arose ***R (Coventry Gliding Club) v Harborough***

---

[57] TCPA 1990, s.78(1)(c)

[58] See ***R (Coventry Gliding Club) v Harborough DC*** [2020] EWHC 3059 (Admin), in which Swift J confirmed that a decision to grant prior approval was a decision *"under the planning acts"* for the purposes of rule 54.5 of the Civil Procedure Rules.

[59] ***F Hoffmann La Roche & Co AG v SSTI*** [1975] AC 295

DC [2020] EWHC 3388 (Admin). Although Swift J did not consider it necessary to determine it, he commented:

> *The facts of this case do not require a decision on the effect of paragraph W(11) in a situation where a decision on an application for prior approval has been taken and communicated within the times permitted, but is then challenged and quashed. Before it became apparent in this case that the Council had not communicated its decision to Mr Garner in the time allowed, the Council had stated that its submission would be that where a decision, properly made and communicated, was quashed the effect of paragraph W(11) was that the right to develop became unconditional because the consequence of the quashing order was that an effective decision had neither been made nor communicated within the 56 day permitted period. Even absent section 3 of the Human Rights Act, I have significant doubts that that conclusion is correct. But if those doubts are misplaced, there would remain a serious issue as to whether such a state of affairs was consistent with the Convention rights of the person who had successfully challenged the prior approval decision. In this instance, however, this matter does not need to be resolved*

59. Whilst persuasive, this judgment is not binding and so the position remains uncertain.

CHAPTER THREE

PART 1 – DEVELOPMENT WITHIN THE CURTILAGE OF A DWELLINGHOUSE[60]

60. Schedule 2, pt.1 of the GPDO is probably one of the most commonly used in practice. It contains a range of rights that can be relied upon to undertake minor works within the curtilage of a dwellinghouse. These are set out below, but first it is necessary to consider what is meant by the words *"dwellinghouse"* and *"curtilage"*.

Dwellinghouse

61. The term *"dwellinghouse"* is not comprehensively defined in the GPDO. Article 2(2) merely states that a *"dwellinghouse"* will not include a building containing one or more flats. A flat is defined in art.2(2) as *"a separate and self-contained set of premises constructed or adapted for use for the purpose of a dwelling and forming part of a building from some other part of which it is divided horizontally"*.

62. In ***Gravesham BC v SSfE*** (1984) 47 P & CR 142, McCullough J explained that whether a building is a dwellinghouse is a question of fact and degree. He provided detailed guidance on the issue:

> *In using a simple word in common usage and leaving it undefined, Parliament realistically expected that, in the overwhelming majority of cases, there would be no difficulty at all in deciding whether a particular building was or was not a dwelling-house. The use in a statute of almost any word in*

[60] Helpful guidance on these rights has been produced by the Ministry of Housing Communities and Local Government: https://assets.publishing.service.gov.uk/government/uploads/system/uploads/attachment_data/file/830643/190910_Tech_Guide_for_publishing.pdf

common usage may give rise to difficulties of interpretation in a very small number of cases, but the problems are both fewer and less troublesome than those that are apt to result when the statute defines the word. The good sense of this is such that I do not intend to resolve the issue that arises in this appeal by attempting to define what Parliament left undefined.

The more helpful approach, in my opinion, is to consider a number of buildings that quite clearly are dwelling-houses and others that equally clearly are not and to see whether this throws up any indication of what ought and what ought not to be taken into account.

Consider a building that anyone would acknowledge was a dwelling-house. If it is not being lived in because, for example, the occupants are on holiday or because they have two houses and spend half the year in each, it remains a dwelling-house. Take a common situation where a family has a second house in the country that is only visited at weekends, in the summer months and for a summer holiday. That is clearly a dwelling-house. So the intention to use one's house, or the practice of using it throughout the year, is not essential.

If a house is empty pending its sale or because its owner cannot, or does not want, to let it, it is still a dwelling-house. So emptiness is not fatal.

If it cannot be occupied because it is flooded, or is undergoing extensive repair, it is still a dwelling-house. So, too, a second home in a remote mountainous district, cut off by snow every winter. So an ability to use it whenever one wants to is not an essential either.

Suppose that there is a national emergency and an order is made prohibiting the use of houses in a particular area for the duration of the emergency: they would nevertheless remain dwelling-houses. So even an inability to use a house lawfully does not necessarily prevent it from being a dwelling-house.

Leaving aside extraordinary events like floods and national emergencies and repairs so extensive that the occupant has to move out, is it a characteristic of every dwelling-house that the owner or occupier could live in it permanently if he wanted to? I think not.

Suppose that a London-based company requires a succession of employees to be based one at a time for four months in a location far distant from London. Suppose that the company buys a house and makes it available to each employee and his family for his tour of duty. It would still be a dwelling-house. Take a holiday cottage subject to time-share with a number of owners each enjoying the right to occupy it for two particular weeks each year. That would still be a dwelling-house.

What have these examples in common? All are buildings that ordinarily afford the facilities required for day-to-day private domestic existence.

This characteristic is lacking in hotels, holiday camps, hostels, residential schools, naval and military barracks and similar places where people may eat, sleep and perhaps spend 24 hours a day. Quite clearly, none of these is a dwelling-house.

Curtilage

63. It will be easy to identify the curtilage of most dwellinghouses (typically the front and back gardens). However, the position is more complex for larger or less typical properties.

64. The term *"curtilage"* is not defined in the GPDO[61] and has been the subject of several judgments. Some assistance can be derived from the *Oxford English Dictionary* definition:

---

[61] Except for specific permitted development rights as set out sch.2, pt.3 where a restrictive definition is provided – see para.X in particular.

> *A small court, yard, garth, or piece of ground attached to a dwelling-house, and forming one enclosure with it, or so regarded by the law; the area attached to and containing a dwelling-house and its out-buildings. Now mostly a legal or formal term, but in popular use in the south-west, where it is pronounced, and often written, courtledge*

65. This is not the end of the story though because to some extent *"curtilage"* not simply an ordinary English word but a legal term of art.[62] In ***Att-Gen x rel Sutcliffe v Calderdale BC*** (1982) 46 P & CR 399, Stephenson LJ identified three factors which must be taken into account in determining what constitutes the curtilage of a building in any given case:

> *Three factors have to be taken into account in deciding whether a structure (or object) is within the curtilage of a listed building ... whatever may be the strict conveyancing interpretation of the ancient and somewhat obscure word 'curtilage'. They are (1) the physical 'layout' of the listed building and the structure, (2) their ownership, past and present, (3) their use or function, past and present. Where they are in common ownership and one is used in connection with the other, there is little difficulty in putting a structure near a building or even some distance from it into its curtilage.*

66. In ***Challenge Fencing v SSHCLG*** [2019] EWHC 553 (Admin), Lieven J (citing other case law) noted that *"an area of land cannot properly be described as a curtilage unless it forms part and parcel of the house or building which it contains or to which it is attached"*. She went on to identify a number of further propositions which should be applied to the question of whether something falls within the curtilage of a building for the purpose of the GPDO:

[62] ***R (Hampshire CC) v SSEFRA*** [2020] EWHC 959 (Admin)

i) The extent of the curtilage of a building is a question of fact and degree, and therefore it must be a matter for the decision-maker, subject to normal principles of public law;

ii) The three Stephenson factors must be taken into account;

a) Physical layout;

b) The ownership past and present;

c) The use or function of the land or buildings, past and present.

iii) A curtilage does not have to be small, but that does not mean that the relative size between the building and its claimed curtilage is not a relevant consideration. Skerritts p.67;

iv) Whether the building or land within the claimed curtilage is ancillary to the main building will be a relevant consideration, but it is not a legal requirement that the claimed curtilage should be ancillary; Skerritts p.67C;

v) The degree to which the building and the claimed curtilage fall within one enclosure is relevant, Sumption at para 17 and the quotation form the OED of curtilage as "A small court, yard or piece of ground attached to a dwelling house and forming one enclosure with it". In my view this will be one aspect of the physical layout, being the first of the Calderdale factors.

vi) The relevant date on which to determine the extent of the curtilage is the date of the application; but this will involve considering both the past history of the site, and how it is laid out and used at the time of the application itself; Sumption at [27]. It appears from Sumption that the Judge considered future intended use of the land or buildings may be relevant, but in my view some care would be needed in applying this proposition to the facts of a particular case. A developer cannot

> *change the curtilage simply by asserting that s/he intends to use the site in a particular way in the future.*

67. In ***R (Hampshire CC) v SSEFRA*** [2020] EWHC 959 (Admin) Holgate J stressed that the factors set out in ***Challenge Fencing*** were not exhaustive and advised practitioners to read the judgment as a whole. He particularly emphasised that when identifying a curtilage (for the purposes of the GPDO) it is not correct to ask whether the land and building together comprise a single unit but rather whether the land is so intimately associated with a building that the land formed part and parcel of the building.

Class A: The enlargement, improvement or other alteration of a dwellinghouse

The scope of the right

68. This right will obviously only apply to work undertaken to a dwellinghouse. In addition, the *"enlargement, improvement or other alteration of a dwellinghouse"* does not include rebuilding.[63] Whether works which purport to be works of enlargement, improvement or alteration in fact amount to rebuilding *"is a question of fact and degree and inevitably fact sensitive"*.[64]

69. To some extent this raises quite a difficult philosophical question – i.e. when does an altered dwellinghouse become a new dwellinghouse?[65] However, the courts have typically dealt with this in a fact-sensitive and practical way. A number of cases dealing with this issue were cited and summarised by Dove J in ***Arnold v SSCLG*** [2015] EWHC 1197 (Admin). It is not possible to derive any clear rules from this analysis, but relevant factors will include the extent of

---

[63] ***Sainty v Minister of Housing and Local Government*** (1964) 15 P. & C.R. 432

[64] ***Arnold v SSCLG*** [2015] EWHC 1197 (Admin) per Dove J at §38

[65] Often referred to as the philosophy of Theseus' Ship or, for the slightly more modern reader, the philosophy of Trigger's Broom – taken from the famous scene in the BBC comedy *Only Fools and Horses*

the works (e.g. the number and size of walls replaced) and the period of time over which the work takes place (e.g. over a few years or several decades). In the following examples the courts have found that works have gone beyond the enlargement, improvement or other alteration of the dwellinghouse:

a. The redevelopment of a house in which only parts of the walls of the western wing of the property were retained;[66]

b. The demolition of two houses and their replacement by houses of different design on slightly different foundations;[67]

c. An operation which involved jacking up the roof, undertaking work on each of the building's four walls and then undertaking work on the roof itself.[68]

70. The creation of basements is capable of falling within Class A, but there will come a point at which the works of excavation, underpinning and support required to create a basement becomes different in character from the enlargement, improvement and alteration of the dwelling and becomes a separate engineering development in itself. Thus, in the context of a terrace house in suburban London, the development of a new basement when there was currently nothing underneath the house, <u>could</u>, as a matter of fact and degree, amount to two substantial developments, because the engineering aspect of excavating a space while supporting the house and the neighbours' properties might be a separate planning aspect.[69]

---

[66] ***Arnold v SSCLG*** [2015] EWHC 1197 (Admin)

[67] ***Sainty v Minister of Housing and Local Government*** (1964) 15 P. & C.R. 432

[68] ***Hewlett v SSE*** [1985] 1 EGLR 170

[69] ***Eatherley v Camden LBC*** [2016] EWHC 3108 (Admin)

71. Finally, it is important to recall two material provisions from s.55 TCPA 1990 which overlap with Class A:

a. Section 55(2)(a) provides that the carrying out for the maintenance, improvement or alteration of any building of works which affect only the interior of the building, or do not materially affect the external appearance of the building, does not amount to development at all and therefore does not even require planning permission. On occasions, where there is a dispute about whether work goes beyond the terms of this section, it will often be concluded that it nevertheless falls within Class A.[70]

b. Section 55(2)(d) provides that the use of any buildings or other land within the curtilage of a dwellinghouse for any purpose incidental to the enjoyment of the dwellinghouse as such will not amount to development. Thus, although development amounting to a change of use will not fall within Class A (which covers operational development), it may well fall within s.55(d). A good example might be the change of use of a detached garage or outbuilding into a home office or a gym.

c. However, this provision does not apply to a change of use involving the subdivision of a single dwellinghouse into two or more dwellinghouses. This would require separate planning permission and does not fall within Class A.[71]

Exceptions

72. Paragraph A.1 sets out a number of circumstances in which the rights under Class A will not be available. These can broadly be divided into exceptions which apply to enlargements, alterations and

---

[70] See, for example, ***Bradford MDC v SSE*** (1977) 35 P&CR 87

[71] TCPA 1990, s.55(3)

improvements generally[72] and exceptions which apply to enlargements (i.e. extensions) specifically.[73]

73. As far as general exceptions are concerned, Class A will not be available where:

a. Permission to use the dwellinghouse as a dwellinghouse has been granted only by virtue of certain other permitted development rights, specifically Class M, N, P, PA or Q of sch.2, pt.3 (changes of use) and Part 20 (construction of new dwellinghouses);[74]

b. As a result of the works, the total area of ground covered by buildings within the curtilage of the dwellinghouse (other than the original dwellinghouse)[75] would exceed 50% of the total area of the curtilage (excluding the ground area of the original dwellinghouse);

c. The height of the part of the dwellinghouse enlarged, improved or altered would exceed the height of the highest part of the roof of the existing dwellinghouse;[76]

---

[72] GPDO, sch.2, pt.1, para.A1(a)-(d), (k)-(l)

[73] GPDO, sch.2, pt.1, para.A1(e)-(ja)

[74] It should be noted that his exception applies to almost all of the rights in sch.2, pt.1

[75] For the purposes of the GPDO "original" means a building as it existed on 1 July 1948 where it was built before that date, and as it was built if built after that date – although slightly different provisions apply to crown land: GPDO, art.2(1)

[76] According to MHCLG guidance, *"the highest part of the roof of the existing house will be the height of the ridge line of the main roof (even though there may be other ridge lines at a lower level) or the height of the highest roof where roofs on a building are flat."*

d. The height of the eaves of the part of the dwellinghouse enlarged, improved or altered would exceed the height of the eaves of the existing[77] dwellinghouse;[78]

e. The development consists of or includes: the construction or provision of a verandah, balcony or raised platform[79], the installation alteration or replacement of a microwave antenna[80], chimney, flue, soil and vent pipe[81]; or an alteration to any part of the roof of the dwellinghouse.[82]

74. As for enlargements, these will not be permitted where:

a. The enlarged part of the dwellinghouse would extend beyond a wall which (i) forms the principal elevation[83] of

---

[77] For the purposes of the GPDO *"existing"* means existing before the carrying out of the development described in the Order: art.2(1)

[78] According to MHCLG guidance the eaves of a house are the point where the lowest point of the roof slope, or a flat roof, meets the outside wall. The height of the eaves is measured from the ground level at the base of the external wall of the extension.

[79] There are defined in the MHCLG guidance as follows: *"A veranda is understood to be a gallery, platform, or balcony, usually roofed and often partly enclosed, extending along the outside of a building at ground level; A balcony is understood to be a platform with a rail, ballustrade or parapet projecting outside an upper storey of a building. A 'Juliet' balcony, where there is no platform and therefore no external access, would normally be permitted development; A raised platform is any platform with a height greater than 0.3 metres and will include roof terraces."*

[80] Meaning a satellite antenna or terrestrial microwave antenna: GPDO, art.2(1). Separate rights exist in relation to these under Class H.

[81] Separate rights for these exist under Class H

[82] Permitted development rights covering work to the roof of a dwellinghouse are contained in Classes B & C (below)

[83] According to MHCLG guidance, *"in most cases the principal elevation will be that part of the house which fronts (directly or at an angle) the main highway serving the house (the main highway will be the one that sets the postcode for the house concerned). It will usually contain the main architectural features such as main bay windows or a porch serving the main entrance to the house. Usually, but not exclusively, the principal elevation will be what is understood to be the front of the house. There will only be one principal*

the original dwellinghouse or (ii) fronts a highway and forms a side elevation of the original dwellinghouse;[84]

b. The enlarged part of the dwellinghouse would be within 2 metres of the boundary of the curtilage of the dwellinghouse, and the height of the eaves of the enlarged part would exceed 3 metres;[85]

75. Different, additional, exceptions apply to single and multi-storey extensions and to side and rear extensions:

a. Multi-storey extensions will only be permitted to walls forming the rear elevation of the original dwellinghouse and where they do not extend beyond wall by more than 3 metres and are more than 7 metres from any boundary of the curtilage which is opposite the rear wall of the dwellinghouse; [86]

b. Single-storey rear extensions will only be permitted where they do not extend beyond the rear wall of the original dwellinghouse by more than 8 metres in the case of a detached dwellinghouse or 6 metres in the case of any other dwellinghouse[87]; or exceed 4 metres in height.[88] In

---

elevation on a house. Where there are two elevations which may have the character of a principal elevation, for example on a corner plot, a view will need to be taken as to which of these forms the principal elevation."

[84] GPDO, Sch.2, pt.1, para.A1(e). According to MHCLG Guidance, the extent to which a building fronts a highway will depend on several factors including: the angle between the elevation and the highway (anything more than 45 degrees will generally not be considered to be fronting a highway); and the distance between the house and the highway (if substantial then the building may not be considered to front a highway).

[85] GPDO, Sch.2, pt.1, para.A1(j)

[86] GPDO, sch.2, pt.1, para.A1(h)

[87] These limits are subject to

[88] GPDO, sch.2, pt.1, para.A1(f)-(g)

order to take advantage of the 8/6 metre extension a developer must also comply with the conditions set out in para.A4, which include a requirement to ask the local planning authority whether prior approval is required. If these conditions are not or cannot be met (or if the development is on art.2(3) land or in a SSSI) then the developer may only extend 4 metres from the original rear elevation, in the case of a detached dwellinghouse, or 3 metres in the case of any other dwellinghouse.

c. Single-storey side extensions will only be permitted where they do not exceed 4 metres in height or have a width greater than half the width of the original dwellinghouse;[89]

d. Any enlargement of a dwellinghouse on art.2(3) land is subject to additional exceptions as set out in para.A2;[90]

e. When considering whether the limits set out above are met, account must be taken of any existing enlargements of the original dwellinghouse.[91] For example, if an original detached dwellinghouse has already been extended to the rear by 4 metres, it cannot be extended any further.

Conditions

76. Paragraphs A3 and A4 impose a number of conditions on development under Class A, including in relation to the exterior materials and placement of any upper floor windows.

---

[89] GPDO, sch.2, pt.1, para.A1(j)

[90] These include a list of proscribed cladding materials. This list is exhaustive and therefore other materials will be permitted.

[91] GPDO, sch.2, pt.1, para.A1(ja)

Class AA: The enlargement of a dwellinghouse by construction of additional storeys

The scope of the right

77. This right was added on 31 August 2020. Its scope is defined in para.AA as follows:

> *The enlargement of a dwellinghouse consisting of the construction of—*
>
> *(a) up to two additional storeys, where the existing dwellinghouse consists of two or more storeys; or*
>
> *(b) one additional storey, where the existing dwellinghouse consists of one storey,*
>
> *immediately above the topmost storey of the dwellinghouse, together with any engineering operations reasonably necessary for the purpose of that construction.*

Exceptions

78. Class AA is subject to a number of exceptions, which are set out in para.AA1. It will not be possible to add any additional storeys where:

    a. Permission to use to dwellinghouse as a dwellinghouse has been granted only by virtue of certain other permitted development rights, specifically Class M, N, O, P, PA or Q of sch.2, pt.3 (changes of use);[92]

    b. The dwellinghouse is located on art.2(3) land or in a SSSI;[93]

---

[92] GPDO, sch.2, pt.1, para.AA1(a)

[93] GPDO, sch.2, pt.1, para.AA1(b)

c. The dwellinghouse was constructed before 1 July 1948 or after 28 October 2018;[94]

d. The dwellinghouse has previously been enlarged by the addition of one or more storeys; [95]

e. The height of the highest part of the roof of the dwellinghouse exceeds 18 metres.[96]

79. Development which falls outside of these exceptions is still subject to quite strict limits:

a. The addition of storeys must not lead the total height of the dwellinghouse to exceed 18 metres;[97]

b. The total height of the existing dwellinghouse must not be increased by more than 3.5 metres where the existing dwellinghouse contains one storey and 7 metres where the existing dwellinghouse contains more than one storey;[98]

c. If the dwellinghouse is not detached, the highest part of the roof must not exceed the height of the building with which it shares a party wall (or if a terrace[99], any building on the row) by more than 3.5 metres;[100]

---

[94] GPDO, sch.2, pt.1, para.AA1(c)

[95] GPDO, sch.2, pt.1, para.AA1(d)

[96] GPDO, sch.2, pt.1, para.AA1(e)

[97] GPDO, sch.2, pt.1, para.AA1(e)

[98] GPDO, sch.2, pt.1, para.AA1(f)

[99] Note that "terrace" is specifically defined for this part in para.AA4 and that this definition differs from that provided for Class B and C at sch.2, pt.2, para.I in that it refers to a row of "buildings" rather than "dwellinghouses".

[100] GPDO, sch.2, pt.1, para.AA1(g)

d. The floor to ceiling height of any additional storey must not exceed the lower of 3 metres or the internal floor to ceiling height of any storey of the principal part[101] of the existing dwellinghouse;[102]

e. Any additional storey must be constructed on the principal part of the dwellinghouse;[103]

f. The development must not include the provision of visible support structures on or attached to the exterior of the dwellinghouse on completion or involve engineering operations other than works within the curtilage of the dwellinghouse to strengthen its existing walls or existing foundations.[104]

Conditions

80. Development under Class AA is subject to a number of conditions, including in relation to external materials, the placement of windows on side elevations and use – the development must be used as a dwellinghouse within the meaning of Class C3 of the UCO or for a use which is ancillary to this.[105]

81. Prior approval is also required as to the impact on the amenity of adjoining premises, the external appearance of the dwellinghouse, air traffic and defence asset implications and the impact on any protected views.[106]

---

[101] *"Principal part"* is defined in para.AA4 as the main part of the dwellinghouse excluding any front, side or rear extension of a lower height, whether this forms part of the original dwellinghouse or is a subsequent addition

[102] GPDO, sch.2, pt.1, para.AA1(h)

[103] GPDO, sch.2, pt.1, para.AA1(i)

[104] GPDO, sch.2, pt.1, para.AA1(j)-(k)

[105] GPDO, sch.2, pt.1, para.AA2(1)-(2)

[106] GPDO, sch.2, pt.1, para.AA2(3)

Classes B & C: Roofs

82. As will be clear from the above, nothing in Class A permits any changes to be made to the roof of the existing building. These are addressed under Classes B & C:

    a. Class B permits *"the enlargement of a dwellinghouse consisting of an addition or alteration to its roof"*

    b. Class C permits *"any other alteration to the roof of a dwellinghouse"*

83. Class B is typically used for loft extensions. It subject to many of the same exceptions as set out above for Class A[107], although the following are of particular note:

    a. Class B may not be relied upon at all where the development is on art.2(3) land;[108]

    b. No part of the dwelling can, as a result of the works, extend beyond the plane of any existing slope which forms the principal elevation of the dwellinghouse and fronts a highway.[109] Thus, put simply, there can be no enlargement of this part of the roof – although it may be possible to add roof lights for a rear loft conversion pursuant to Class C (see below);

    c. The cubic content[110] of the resulting roof space would exceed the cubic content of the original roof space by

[107] See GPDO, sch.2, pt.1, para.B1(a),(b)&(e).

[108] GPDO, sch.2, pt.1, para.B1(f)

[109] GPDO, sch.2, pt.1, para.B1(c)

[110] Defined in art.2(1) GPDO as the cubic content of a structure or building measured externally

more than 40 cubic metres for a terrace house[111] or 50 cubic metres in any other case.[112] Resulting roof space means the roof space as enlarged, taking into account any enlargement to the original[113] roof space.[114] In addition, *"roof space"* does not mean the void between the ceiling of the highest room and the roof, but rather roof itself (as measured externally).[115]

d. Class B may not be relied upon where permission to construct or use the dwellinghouse has been granted under specified provisions of the GPDO.[116]

84. Prior approval is not required for development under Class B, but other conditions apply, including in relation to the materials, the relationship between the development and the existing eaves and the types of windows which may be installed.[117]

85. Class C is subject to similar exceptions to Class B (insofar as they are relevant to alteration as opposed to enlargement), although the following points of difference are of note:

---

[111] A terrace house means a dwellinghouse situated in a row of 3 or more dwellinghouses used or designed for use as single dwellings, where (a) it shares a party wall with, or has a main wall adjoining the main wall of, the dwellinghouse on either side or (b) if it is at the end of a row, it shares a party wall with or has a main wall adjoining the main wall of a dwellinghouse which fulfils the requirements of sub-paragraph (a): GPDO, sch.2, pt.1, para.I

[112] GPDO, sch.2, pt.1, para.B1(d)

[113] i.e. the roof space as built or as it existed on 1 July 1948

[114] GPDO, sch.2, pt.1, para.B3

[115] ***Havering LBC v SSCLG*** [2017] EWHC 1546 (Admin)

[116] GPDO, sch.2, pt.1, para.B1(a),(g)-(l)

[117] GPDO, sch.2, pt.1, para.B2. More detail about the application of these conditions is given in the MHCLG guidance

a. Development under Class C may take place on art.2(3) land;[118]

b. Development under Class C will not be permitted where the alteration would protrude more than 0.15 metres beyond the plane of the slope of the original roof when measured from the perpendicular with the external surface of the original roof.[119] Thus, for example, a skylight may be installed on a roof provided it does not project more than 0.15 metres;

c. Class C does not permit the installation alteration or replacement of solar photovoltaics or solar thermal equipment.[120]

Class D: Porches

86. Class D permits *"the erection or construction of a porch outside any external door of a dwellinghouse"*. It is subject to several exceptions which are set out in para.D1. They include limits on the size and location of any porch: the ground area (measured externally) must not exceed 3 square metres; no part of the structure can be more than 3 metres above ground level or within 2 metres of the boundary between the curtilage of the dwellinghouse and a highway.

Class E: Buildings etc incidental to the enjoyment of a dwellinghouse

The scope of the right

87. Class E permits:

> *The provision within the curtilage of the dwellinghouse of—*

---

[118] GPDO, sch.2, pt.1, para.C1

[119] GPDO, sch.2, pt.1, para.C1(b)

[120] GPDO, sch.2, pt.1, para.C1(b). This is provided for separately under sch.2, pt.14.

(a) any building or enclosure, swimming or other pool required for a purpose incidental to the enjoyment of the dwellinghouse as such, or the maintenance, improvement or other alteration of such a building or enclosure; or

(b) a container used for domestic heating purposes for the storage of oil or liquid petroleum gas.

88. Class E permits the provision of a specified list of structures or features within the curtilage of a dwellinghouse. The term *"building"* is defined in art.2(1), broadly, as including any part of a building and any structure or erection, but not including mechanical plant or machinery or gates, fences, walls, or other means of enclosure. This definition also indicates that *"enclosure"* (which is not separately defined in the GPDO) includes gates, fences and walls. The term *"swimming pool"* is unlikely to cause much difficulty. The term *"pool"* is not defined, but is likely to include ponds.

89. To fall within the scope of the above right all of these structures and features must be required for a purpose which is *"incidental"* to the enjoyment of the dwellinghouse as a dwellinghouse or to the maintenance, improvement or other alteration of such a building or enclosure.

90. Whether or not something is incidental to the enjoyment of a dwellinghouse is not straightforward. The position of the MHCLG is that a use cannot be *"incidental"* to residential use if it constitutes residential use.[121] Thus, Class E cannot be used for the construction of a separate dwellinghouse. Nor, though, can it be used to erect something which will be used for primary living accommodation, such as a bedroom, bathroom or kitchen. At the other end of the spectrum, the use cannot be so far removed from residential use as to not be considered *"incidental"* to it. The test is whether the

[121] See the MHCLG technical guidance

building or enclosure is reasonably required for a purpose incidental to the enjoyment of a particular dwellinghouse. It is one of *"objective reasonableness"*[122] and a matter of fact and degree in every case. Relevant factors will include the nature and impact of the use, the size of the structure and whether it has separate access. Some helpful illustrations are as follows:

a. The provision of buildings for pottery, billiards and indoor archery has been found to be capable of falling within Class E;[123]

b. The erection of a study room or home office is capable of falling within Class E, but will not do so in every case;[124]

c. The keeping of poultry, bees, pet animals, birds or other livestock for the domestic needs or personal enjoyment of the occupants of the dwellinghouse will fall within Class E;[125]

d. The erection of an aircraft hangar is very unlikely to fall within Class E and indeed may not be capable of doing so.[126]

91. In truth, though, this remains a grey area and any developer who has concern about whether proposed development would fall under Class E would be wise to apply to their local planning authority for a certificate of lawful proposed use or development before embarking on any construction.

92. A further complicating factor is the fact that s.55(2)(f) of the TCPA 1990 does allow for the change of use of a building to another use

---

[122] See ***Wallington v Secretary of State for Wales*** (1990) 62 P&CR 150

[123] ***Emin v SSE*** (1989) 58 P&CR 416

[124] ***Peche d'or Investments v SSE*** [1996] JPL 311

[125] GPDO, sch.2, pt.1, para.E4

[126] ***Secretary of State for Transport v Thurrock BC*** [2002] EWCA Civ 226

within the same use class. This would include a change of use from an incidental to a primary residential use. It may therefore be possible to erect a building for incidental residential use (e.g. a tool store) and then change the use to a primary one (e.g. a bedroom). However, great care should be taken. If there was never any true intention of using the building for the incidental use then this would be a *"sham"* of the type which the Court of Appeal has found would clearly fall outside of Class E.[127] There would need to have been more than nominal incidental use before the change took place – likely lasting at least several months if not more.[128]

93. It should be noted that Class E also permits the erection of a container for domestic heating purposes. This does not technically need to be incidental to the use of the dwellinghouse, but the capacity of the container cannot exceed 3,500 litres.[129]

Exceptions

94. Class E is subject to several exceptions, which include:

    a. Class E may not be relied upon within the curtilage of a listed building;[130]

    b. No part of the building, enclosure, pool or container would be situated on land forward of a wall forming the principal elevation of the original dwellinghouse;[131]

    c. The total area of ground covered by buildings, enclosures and containers within the curtilage (other than the original dwellinghouse) cannot exceed 50% of the total

---

[127] ***Rambridge v SSE*** (1997) 74 P&CR 126

[128] See, for example, ***Kwik Save Discount Group v SSW*** [1981] JPL 198

[129] GPDO, sch.2, pt.1, para.E1(j)

[130] GPDO, sch.2, pt.1, para.E1(g)

[131] GPDO, sch.2, pt.1, para.E1(c)

area of the curtilage (excluding the ground area of the original dwellinghouse);[132]

d. The building cannot have more than a single storey;[133]

e. The height of the building, enclosure or container cannot exceed

    i. 4 metres in the case of a building with a dual-pitched roof,

    ii. 2.5 metres in the case of a building, enclosure or container within 2 metres of the boundary of the curtilage of the dwellinghouse, or

    iii. 3 metres in any other case;[134]

f. The height of the eaves of the building cannot exceed 2.5 metres;[135]

g. The works carried out cannot include the construction or provision of a verandah, balcony or raised platform or relate to a dwelling or microwave antenna;[136]

h. Where the land within the curtilage of the dwellinghouse is in an AONB, the Broads, a National Park or a World Heritage Site, development is not permitted by Class E if the total area of ground covered by buildings, enclosures, pools and containers situated more than 20 metres from

---

[132] GPDO, sch.2, pt.1, para.E1(b)

[133] GPDO, sch.2, pt.1, para.E1(c)

[134] GPDO, sch.2, pt.1, para.E1(d)

[135] GPDO, sch.2, pt.1, para.E1(f)

[136] GPDO, sch.2, pt.1, para.E1(h)-(i)

any wall of the dwellinghouse would exceed 10 square metres;[137]

i. Where the land within the curtilage of the dwellinghouse is in art.2(3) land, development is not permitted by Class E if any part of the building, enclosure, pool or container would be situated on land between a wall forming a side elevation of the dwellinghouse and the boundary of the curtilage of the dwellinghouse;[138]

j. Class E may not be relied upon where permission to construct or use the dwellinghouse has been granted under specified provisions of the GPDO.[139]

Class F: Hard surfaces incidental to the enjoyment of a dwellinghouse

95. Class F permits development consisting of:

> *(a) the provision within the curtilage of a dwellinghouse of a hard surface for any purpose incidental to the enjoyment of the dwellinghouse as such; or*
>
> *(b) the replacement in whole or in part of such a surface.*

96. The GPDO does not contain any definition of hard surface, although it ought not to be too difficult to identify in practice. In fact, this is a fairly broad right and could cover not just the hard surfacing of a driveway, or the laying of a patio, but also, potentially the construction of a basketball court provided that it is incidental to the enjoyment of the dwellinghouse as such (as to which see above). There is also no limit on the amount of the curtilage that can be hard surfaced. The construction of raised patios is a frequent source of planning disputes. If the height of the patio exceeds 0.3

[137] GPDO, sch.2, pt.1, para.E2

[138] GPDO, sch.2, pt.1, para.E3

[139] GPDO, sch.2, pt.1, para.E1(a)&(k)

metres it will amount to a *"raised platform"* and will fall outside the scope of the GPDO.[140]

97. As with many of the other rights in pt.1, para.F1 includes an exception where permission to construct or use the dwellinghouse has been granted under specified provisions of the GPDO.[141] Additional conditions also apply where the surface will be situated on land forming the principal elevation of the dwellinghouse and a highway.[142]

Class H: Microwave antenna on a dwellinghouse

98. Class H permits *"the installation, alteration or replacement of a microwave antenna on a dwellinghouse or within the curtilage of a dwellinghouse."*

99. Para.H1 imposes limits on the type and number of antenna that can be installed:

    a. Antenna cannot be installed under Class H if it would result in more than two antennas being on or within the curtilage of the dwellinghouse;[143]

    b. No antenna with a cubic capacity in excess of 35 litres or exceeding 1 metre in length (reducing to 0.6 metres where the antenna is placed on a chimney) may be installed;[144]

---

[140] GPDO, sch.2, pt.1, para.I

[141] GPDO, sch.2, pt.1, para.F1

[142] GPDO, sch.2, pt.1, para.F2

[143] GPDO, sch.2, pt.1, para.H1(b)

[144] GPDO, sch.2, pt.1, para.H1(b)

c. No antenna may protrude above the height of a chimney, if placed on one, or the highest part of the roof if not;[145]

100. Additional limits are imposed for art.2(3) land and Class H may not be used where permission to construct or use the dwellinghouse has been granted under specified provisions of the GPDO.[146]

101. Paragraph H2 imposes conditions which require any antenna installed on a building to be sited so far as practicable to minimise its effect on the external appearance of the building. In addition, any antenna which is no longer needed for reception or transmission purpose must be removed as soon as reasonably practicable.

---

145 GPDO, sch.2, pt.1, para.H1(b)-(c)

146 GPDO, sch.2, pt.1, para.H1(a),(e)&(f)

CHAPTER FOUR

PART 2 – MINOR OPERATIONS

102. Part 2 provides for various types of minor operational development.

Class A: Gates, fences, walls etc

103. Class A permits the *"erection, construction, maintenance, improvement or alteration of a gate, fence, wall or other means of enclosure"*.

104. The words *"means of enclosure"* are key here. Any gate, fence or wall must enclose or contribute to the enclosure of something. This is a question of fact and degree, and some gaps maybe permitted[147] – although a freestanding wall or gate in the middle of a garden would not be permitted under Class A.[148] The right is not restricted to walls gates or fences and can include structures which are of a similar character.

105. Class A cannot be relied upon to carry out development within the curtilage of, or to any means of enclosure surrounding, a listed building.[149] Paragraph A1 also imposes a number of restrictions on the height of any means of enclosure:

a. No means of enclosure can exceed 2 metres above ground level in any case;

b. Where it is constructed adjacent to a highway used by vehicular traffic, it cannot exceed 2 meters above ground level for a school (provided it does not obstruct the view

---

147 ***Wycombe DC v SSE*** [1994] EGCS 61

148 ***Oxfordshire DC v SSSE*** (1986) 52 P&CR 1

149 GPDO, sch.2, pt.2, para.A1(d)

of users of the highway) or 1 metre above ground level in any other case;

c. Where the work merely involves maintenance, improvement or alteration the height of the means of enclosure cannot exceed the greater of its existing height or the limits set out in (a) and (b) above.

Class B: Means of access to a highway

106. Class B permits *"the formation, laying out and construction of a means of access to a highway which is not a trunk road or a classified road, where that access is required in connection with development permitted by any Class in this Schedule (other than by Class A of this Part)"*.

107. This right is subject to art.3(6) GPDO which prohibits reliance on the Order to create an obstruction to the view of persons using any highway used by vehicular traffic, so as to be likely to cause a danger to such persons. Access which does not open directly onto a highway may still be permitted where it can reasonably be considered to provide a means of access to the highway (i.e. via a service road).[150]

Class C: Exterior painting

108. Class C permits *"the painting of the exterior of any building or work"* but does not extend to painting for the purposes of advertisement, announcement or direction.[151] Painting is defined as including *"any application of colour"*.[152]

Classes D&E: Charging for electric vehicles

109. Class D permits *"the installation, alteration or replacement, within an area lawfully used for off-street parking, of an electrical outlet mounted*

---

[150] For example, see ***James v SSW*** (1996) 76 P&CR 52

[151] GPDO, sch.2, pt.2, para.C1

[152] GPDO, sch.2, pt.2, para.C2

on a wall for recharging electric vehicles." Such development is likely to become increasingly common, although Class D may not be relied upon within designated ancient monuments and the curtilage of listed buildings. Outlets are also subject to restrictions on their size and location, and must be removed where no longer in use.[153]

110. Class E permits *"the installation, alteration or replacement, within an area lawfully used for off-street parking, of an upstand with an electrical outlet mounted on it for recharging electric vehicles"*. It is subject to similar restrictions to Class D.[154]

Class F: Closed circuit television cameras

111. Class F permits *"the installation, alteration or replacement on a building of a closed circuit television camera to be used for security purposes."* This right is subject to a number of restrictions on the placement, location and number of cameras.[155] In addition, each camera must be sited so as to minimise its effect on the external appearance of the building. Cameras must be removed once they are no longer required for security purposes.

---

[153] GPDO, sch.2, pt.2, paras.D1-D2

[154] GPDO, sch.2, pt.2, paras.E1-E2

[155] GPDO, sch.2, pt.2, paras.F1-F2

CHAPTER FIVE

PART 3 – CHANGES OF USE

112. Part 3 is comfortably the longest section of the GPDO. It has also been extensively covered in another work.[156] As explained above, the UCO provides that a change of use within a particular use class will not amount to development at all. However, part 3 permits changes between different use classes. A summary of the permitted changes can be found in the following table.

Prior approval needed?	No	No
Applies to SSSI	Yes	Yes
Applies to article 2(3) land	Yes	Yes
Applies to listed building	Yes	Yes
To (Use Class as per UCO)	A1 (shops)/A2 (financial and professional services)	A4 (drinking establishments) and *vice versa*
From (Use class as per UCO)	A3 (restaurants and cafes/A5 (hot food takeaways)	A4/A3 (drinking establishments with expanded food provision)
GPDO, sch.2, pt.3, Class	A	AA

[156] Martin Goodall, *A practical guide to permitted changes of use under the General Permitted Development Order* (3rd edn, Oxford 2019).

No	Yes	No	No	No	No
Yes	No	Yes	Yes	Yes	Yes
Yes	Yes	Yes	Yes	Yes	Yes
Yes	No	Yes	Yes	Yes	Yes
A3 (restaurants and cafes)	A3 (restaurants and cafes)	A2 (financial and professional services)	A1 (shops)	A2 (financial and professional services)	Mixed use: A1 (shops), A2 (financial and professional services), betting office or pay day loan shop or casino, C3 (dwellinghouse)
A5 (hot food takeaways)	A1 (shops), A2 (financial and professional services), betting office or pay day loan shop or casino	A1 (shops)	A2 (financial and professional services), betting office or pay day loan shop	Betting office or pay day loan shop	A1 (shops), A2 (financial and professional services), betting office or pay day loan shop
B	C	D	E	F	G

No	No	Yes	Yes	No	No
Yes	Yes	No	No	Yes	Yes
Yes	Yes	No	No	Yes	Yes
Yes	Yes	No	No	Yes	Yes
A1 (shops), A2 (financial and professional services), betting office or pay day loan shop	B1 (business) B8 (storage or distribution)	D2 (assembly and leisure)	B1(a) (offices)	D2 (assembly and leisure)	C3 (dwellinghouse) or C4 (house in multiple occupation)
Mixed use: A1 (shops), A2 (financial and professional services), betting office or pay day loan shop, C3 (dwellinghouse) mixed use	B2 (general industrial) or B8 (storage or distribution) B1 (business) or B2 (general industrial)	A1 (shops), A2 (financial and professional services), betting office or pay day loan	A1 (shops), A2 (financial and professional services), A5 (hot food takeaway), betting office or pay day loan,	Casino	C3 (dwellinghouse) or C4 (house in multiple occupation)
H	I	J	JA	K	L

Yes	Yes	Yes	Yes	Yes	Yes
No	No	No	Yes	No	No
No	Some[157]	Some	Yes	Some	Yes
No	No	No	No	No	No
C3 (dwellinghouse)	C3 (dwellinghouses)	C3 (dwellinghouses)	C3 (dwellinghouses)	C3 (dwellinghouses)	C3 (dwellinghouses)
Mixed use: A1 (shops), A2 (financial and professional services), A5 (hot food takeaway), betting office or [illegible]	E (commercial business and service)	Casinos/amusem ent arcades	B1(a) offices	B8 (storage and distribution)	B1(c) (light industrial)
M	MA	N	O	P	PA

[157] i.e. some land falling within the definition of article 2(3) land is excluded.

Yes	Yes	Yes	Yes	Yes
No	Yes	No	Yes	Yes
No	Yes	Yes	Yes	Yes
No	No	No	No	No
C3 (dwellinghouses)	Flexible: A1 (shops), A2 (financial and professional services), A3 (restaurants and cafes), B1 (business), B8 (storage and distribution), C1 (hotels), D2 (assembly and leisure)	State funded school or registered nursery	State funded school or registered nursery	Previous lawful use prior to change under Class T
Agricultural building	Agricultural building	Agricultural building	B1 (business), C1 (hotels), C2 (residential institutions), C2A (secure residential institutions) or D2 (assembly and	State funded school or registered nursery
Q	R	S	T	U

CHAPTER SIX

PART 4 – TEMPORARY BUILDINGS AND USES

113. This part of the GPDO permits operational development and changes of use which are associated with temporary buildings and uses of land. These rights have been extended during the "lockdown" associated with the outbreak of Covid-19, principally to assist businesses maintain "social distancing".[158] It remains to be seen whether they will persevere beyond the "lockdown", but on the assumption that they will not, they are not discussed below.

Class A: Temporary buildings and structures

114. Class A permits *"the provision on land of buildings, moveable structures, works, plant or machinery required temporarily in connection with and for the duration of operations being or to be carried out on, in, under or over that land or on land adjoining that land."*

115. This is not a freestanding right and can only be used in connection with other operational development being carried out on, in, under or over the land concerned or adjoining land. This development must be lawful and must not constitute mining operations.[159]

116. In ***R (Wilsdon) v First Secretary of Sate*** [2006] EWHC 2980 (Admin), Sullivan J gave guidance as to how to determine whether a building or structure is *"required temporarily"*. He found that this will be a question of fact and degree but that the requirement for the building or structure must be reasonable. The size and means of construction of the building or structure will be relevant factors: the larger and more permanent it is, the less likely that is genuinely

[158] See Classes BA and DA in particular.

[159] GPDO, sch.2, pt.4, para.A1

required temporarily – although it might in some cases be reasonable to construct a permanent building for a temporary purpose. Paragraph A2 imposes a condition requiring the removal of the building and structure and reinstatement of the land once the associated operations have been carried out.

Class B: Temporary use of land

117. Class B permits:

> *The use of any land for any purpose for not more than 28 days in total in any calendar year, of which not more than 14 days in total may be for the purposes of—*
>
> *(a) the holding of a market;*
>
> *(b) motor car and motorcycle racing including trials of speed, and practising for these activities,*
>
> *and the provision on the land of any moveable structure for the purposes of the permitted use.*

118. It will often be difficult to distinguish between a temporary and a permanent use. However, if a local planning authority is satisfied that the developer intends to make a permanent change of use (or one which exceeds the relevant time limit in Class C) then it may enforce against it even before the time limit has expired.[160]

119. Class B is not available where the land in question is a listed building or within the curtilage of a listed building or where the use of the land is for a caravan site.[161] Use of land for the purposes of advertisement is also prohibited.[162] Additional uses are prohibited for land within a SSSI, namely:

---

[160] ***Miller-Mead v MHCLG*** [1963] 2 QB 196

[161] This is provided for separately under sch.2, pt.5

[162] GPDO, sch.2, pt.4, para.B1(e)

a. Motor car and motorcycle racing including trials of speed or other motor sports, and practising for these activities;

b. Clay pigeon shooting; or

c. Any war game.[163]

Class C: Use as a state-funded school for 2 academic years

120. Class C permits *"the use of a building and any land within its curtilage as a state-funded school for 2 academic years"*. A state funded school is defined in para.C3 as *"a school funded wholly or mainly from public funds"*. This right is subject to several exceptions and (reassuringly) will not apply where the site in question is or forms part of a military explosives storage area, safety hazard area or a pub.[164]

Class D: Shops, financial, cafes, takeaways etc to temporary flexible use

121. Class D provides for the change of use from a number of specified use classes to a *"flexible use"* within a specified list of use classes for a single continuous period up to three years. *"Flexible use"* is defined in para.D3 as *"use of any building or land for a use falling within the list of uses set out in Class D(b) and change of use (in accordance with Class D) between any use in that list"*.

122. Paragraph D1 sets some restrictions on the amount of floor space and the type/location of buildings to which this right will apply. This

---

[163] GPDO, sch.2, pt.4, para.B1(d). *"War game"* is defined in para.F as *"an enacted, mock or imaginary battle conducted with weapons which are designed not to injure (including smoke bombs, or guns or grenades which fire or spray paint or are otherwise used to mark other participants), but excludes military activities or training exercises organised by or with the authority of the Secretary of State for Defence"*

[164] GPDO, sch.2, pt.4, para.C1

right is also subject to a number of conditions, including a requirement to notify the local planning authority in advance.[165]

Class E: Temporary use of buildings of land for film-making purposes

123. The use of land (other than a purpose built studio) for filming for any material period of time is likely to amount to a change of use of that land requiring planning permission. Class E provides for this by permitting:

> *Development consisting of—*
>
> *(a) the temporary use of any land or buildings for a period not exceeding 9 months in any 27 month period for the purpose of commercial film-making; and*
>
> *(b) the provision on such land, during the filming period, of any temporary structures, works, plant or machinery required in connection with that use.*

124. This is subject to a number of exceptions. The land in question cannot be used for overnight accommodation or exceed 1.5 hectares.[166] Limits are also placed on the height of temporary structures, works, plant or machinery.[167] Class E is also not available on certain types of land such as art.2(3) land or land within the curtilage of a listed building.[168]

125. Prior approval is also required for Class E.[169]

[165] GPDO, sch.2, pt.4, para.D2.

[166] GPDO, sch.2, pt.4, para.E1(a)&(b)

[167] GPDO, sch.2, pt.4, para.E(c)

[168] GPDO, sch.2, pt.4, para.E(d)-(g)

[169] GPDO, sch.2, pt.4, para.E3

CHAPTER SEVEN

PART 5 – CARAVAN SITES

126. Part 5 provides various rights in relation to caravan sites, although it must be remembered that permanent caravan sites also require licences pursuant to the Caravan Sites Control of Development Act 1960 ("the 1960 Act").

Class A: Use of land as a caravan site

127. Class A permits the use of land, other than a building, as a caravan site in the circumstances specified in paras. 2-10 of sch.1 to the 1960 Act, which are, broadly:

a. Use by a person travelling with a caravan for one or two nights;

b. Use of holdings of five acres or more in certain circumstances;

c. Sites occupied and supervised by certain exempted organisations;[170]

d. Sites approved by exempted organisations;

e. Meetings organised by exempted organisations;

f. Agricultural and forestry workers;

g. Building and engineering sites; and

---

[170] i.e. an organisation which has been granted a certificate by the Secretary of State stating that he is satisfied that its objects include the encouragement or promotion of recreational activities: 1960 Act, sch.1, para.12

h. Travelling showmen (excluding use for winder quarters).

128. *"Caravan"* is defined in art.2(1) GPDO as having the same meaning as for the purposes of pt.1 of the 1960 Act, namely any structure designed or adapted for human habitation which is capable of being moved from one place to another (whether by being towed, or by being transported on a motor vehicle or trailer) and any motor vehicle so designed or adapted bit not including railway rolling stock which is on rails or any tent.[171] *"Caravan site"* is defined in art.2(1) GPDO as *"land on which a caravan is stationed for the purposes of human habitation and land which is used in conjunction with land on which a caravan is so stationed."*

129. Where the circumstances set out above cease to exist the use must be discontinued and all caravans removed as soon as reasonably practicable.[172] Many caravan sites, of course, do not just include caravans but infrastructure, pathways and services. In these circumstances, the mere removal of caravans may not be sufficient to amount to a discontinuation of use. As ever, it will be a question of fact and degree.[173]

Class B: Development on caravan site required by conditions

130. Class B simply permits development which is required by the conditions of a site licence being in force under the 1960 Act, further demonstrating the overlap between planning control and licensing in this area.

---

[171] 1960 Act, s.29(1)

[172] GPDO, sch.2, pt.5, para.A1

[173] ***R (Hall Hunter) v FSS*** [2006] EWHC 3482 (Admin)

Class C: Use of land by members of certain recreational organisations

131. Class C permits the use of land by members of a recreational organisation for the purposes of recreation or instruction, and the erection or placing of tents on the land for the purposes of the use, except where the land or building is within the curtilage of a dwellinghouse. A *"recreational organisation"* is an organisation holding a certificate of exemption under section 269 of the Public Health Act 1936 (power of local authority to control use of moveable dwellings).[174] At present, these include the Scout Association, Girl Guides, Army Cadet Force Association and the Camping and Caravan Club. In essence, this allows for a small group of trusted organisations to erect campsites without applying for planning permission.

[174] GPDO, sch.2, pt.5, para.C2

CHAPTER EIGHT

PART 6 – AGRICULTURE AND FORESTRY

132. It important to recall that the use of land for the purposes of agriculture or forestry is not *"development"* for the purpose of s.55 of the TCPA 1990.[175] Part 6 therefore deals with operational development which is reasonably required for the use of land as such.

Class A: Agricultural development on units of 5 hectares or more

133. Class A applies only to larger agricultural units. It permits:

> *The carrying out on agricultural land comprised in an agricultural unit of 5 hectares or more in area of—*
>
> *(a) works for the erection, extension or alteration of a building; or*
>
> *(b) any excavation or engineering operations,*
>
> *which are reasonably necessary for the purposes of agriculture within that unit.*

The scope of the right

134. *"Agriculture"* is not defined in GPDO, but is defined in the TCPA 1990 as follows:

> *agriculture includes horticulture, fruit growing, seed growing, dairy farming, the breeding and keeping of livestock (including any creature kept for the production of food, wool, skins or fur, or for the purpose of its use in the farming of land), the use of*

---

[175] TCPA 1990, s.55(2)(e)

land as grazing land, meadow land, osier land, market gardens and nursery grounds, and the use of land for woodlands where that use is ancillary to the farming of land for other agricultural purposes, and agricultural shall be construed accordingly.

135. *"Agricultural land"* is defined in the GPDO as *"land which, before development permitted by this Part is carried out, is land in use for agriculture and which is so used for the purposes of a trade or business, and excludes any dwellinghouse or garden"*[176]

136. *"Agricultural unit"* is defined in the same provision as meaning *"agricultural land which is occupied as a unit for the purposes of agriculture, including (a) any dwelling or other building on that land occupied for the purpose of farming the land by the person who occupies the unit; or (b) any dwelling on that land occupied by a farmworker."*

137. Whether development is *"reasonably necessary"* for the purposes of agriculture will be a question of fact and degree. However, the GPDO states that, for the purpose of Class A, such development will include *"the erection, extension or alteration of a building, for housing a biomass boiler or an anaerobic digestion system; for storage of fuel for or waste from that boiler or system; or for housing a hydro-turbine."*[177]

Exceptions

138. Class A is subject to a number of exceptions:

a. It will not apply at all where the development in question will be carried out on a separate parcel of land forming part of the agricultural unit which is less than 1 hectare in area. [178] Whether land forms a *"separate parcel of land"* is a matter of fact and degree, which is likely to depend

[176] GPDO, sch.2, pt.6, para.D1(1)

[177] GPDO, sch.2, pt.6, para.D1(7)

[178] GPDO, sch.2, pt.6, para.A1(a)

quite heavily on the nature of any boundary or separation between it and the rest of the unit.[179];

b. It will not apply where the development would consist of the erection or extension of any agricultural building on an established agricultural unit (as defined in pt.3, para.X) where development under Class Q (change of use from agricultural building to dwellinghouse) or S (change of use from agricultural buildings to school or nursery) of sch.2, pt.3 has been carried out within a period of 10 years ending with the date on which development under Class A(a) begins;

c. It does permit work which would consist of or include the erection, extension or alteration of a dwelling.[180] Nor does it permit the provision of a building, structure or works not designed for agricultural purposes.[181] This latter restriction is more about appearance than function. In other words, a barn constructed under Class A must look like a barn, rather than, for example, a dwellinghouse;[182]

d. It poses various restrictions on the ground area which will be covered, the height of any building, structure or works;[183]

---

179 ***Tyack v SSE*** (1989) 57 P & CR 140

180 GPDO, sch.2, pt.6, para.A1(c)

181 GPDO, sch.2, pt.6, para.A1(d)

182 See ***Green v SSE*** [1985] JPL 323 for an example of an attempt by farmer to erect a "calf-rearing building" which bore a suspicious resemblance to a dwellinghouse

183 GPDO, sch.2, pt.6, para.A1(e)-(g)

e. No part of the development may take place within 25 metres of a metalled part of a trunk road or classified road;[184]

f. It does not permit the erection of or any work to a building structure or excavation used or to be used for the accommodation of livestock or for the storage of sewage sludge where the building structure or excavation is or would be within 400m of a protected building.[185] A *"protected building"* means *"any permanent building which is normally occupied by people or would be so occupied, if it were in use for purposes for which it is designed; but does not include: (a) a building within the agricultural unit; or (b) a dwelling or other building on another agricultural unit which is used for or in connection with agriculture"*; [186]

g. It cannot involve excavations or engineering operations which are connected with fish farming on or over land defined in art.2(4) GPDO;[187]

h. It cannot be used to erect any building for storing fuel for or waste from a biomass boiler or anaerobic digestion system in certain circumstances.[188]

Conditions

139. Development carried out under Class A will be subject to a number of conditions about the use and movement of certain waste materials. In addition prior approval must be sought for certain specified work involving the erection, extension or alteration of a building and the

---

[184] GPDO, sch.2, pt.6, para.A1(h)

[185] GPDO, sch.2, pt.6, para.A1(i)

[186] GPDO, sch.2, pt.6, para.D1(1)

[187] GPDO, sch.2, pt.6, para.A1(j)

[188] GPDO, sch.2, pt.6, para.A1(k)

formation or alteration of a private way.[189] Para.A2 also applies conditions relation to *"the significant extension"* or *"significant alteration"* of a building.[190] These are defined as meaning *"any extension or alteration, as the case may be, of the building where the cubic content of the original building would be exceeded by more than 10% or the height of the building as extended or altered would exceed the height of the original building"*.[191]

Class B: Agricultural development on units of less than 5 hectares

140. Class B permits:

> *The carrying out on agricultural land comprised in an agricultural unit, of not less than 0.4 but less than 5 hectares in area, of development consisting of—*
>
> *(a) the extension or alteration of an agricultural building;*
>
> *(b) the installation of additional or replacement plant or machinery;*
>
> *(c) the provision, rearrangement or replacement of a sewer, main, pipe, cable or other apparatus;*
>
> *(d) the provision, rearrangement or replacement of a private way;*
>
> *(e) the provision of a hard surface;*
>
> *(f) the deposit of waste; or*
>
> *(g) the carrying out of any of the following operations in connection with fish farming, namely, repairing ponds and raceways; the installation of grading machinery, aeration*

---

[189] GPDO, sch.2, pt.6, para.A2

[190] GPDO, sch.2, pt.6, para.A2(4)-(5)

[191] GPDO, sch.2, pt.6, para.D1

equipment or flow meters and any associated channel; the dredging of ponds; and the replacement of tanks and nets,

where the development is reasonably necessary for the purposes of agriculture within the unit.

141. Class B is subject to a number of exceptions and conditions which are similar in nature, but not necessarily in substance, to those which apply to Class A.[192]

Class C: Mineral working for agricultural purposes

142. Class C permits *"the winning and working on land held or occupied with land used for the purposes of agriculture of any minerals reasonably necessary for agricultural purposes within the agricultural unit of which it forms part."* It may not be relied upon where excavation would be made within 25 metres of a metalled part of a trunk road or classified road.[193] A condition significantly limits where any minerals taken extracted from the land may be moved to.[194]

Class E: Forestry development

143. The rights provided under Class E are similar in nature and extent to those provided under Classes A and B.

---

[192] GPDO, sch.2, pt.6, paras.B2-B5

[193] GPDO, sch.2, pt.6, para.C1

[194] GPDO, sch.2, pt.6, para.C1

CHAPTER NINE

PART 7 – NON-DOMESTIC EXTENSIONS, ALTERATIONS, ETC

144. Part 7 authorises a very wide range of non-domestic development. The relevant rights, limitations and conditions are set out in the GPDO and have not been the subject of significant legal dispute in and of themselves. They can be broadly summarised as follows:

   a. Class A: the extension or alteration of a shop or financial or professional services establishment, subject to limitations including on the size and location;

   b. Class B: the erection or construction of a trolley store within the curtilage of a shop;

   c. Class C: development consisting of the erection or construction of a collection facility within the curtilage of a shop;

   d. Class D: development consisting of modification of a loading bay of a shop. *"Loading bay"* is defined as *"any facility, including vehicle ramps, for the loading or unloading of goods vehicles;"*[195]

   e. Class E: development consisting of the provision of a hard surface within the curtilage of a shop or catering, financial or professional services establishment or the replacement in whole or part of such a surface;

---

[195] GPDO, sch.2, pt.7, para.D3

f. Class F: the extension or alteration of an office building, subject to limitations including on the size and location;

g. Class G: development consisting of the provision of a hard surface within the curtilage of an office building to be used for the purpose of the office concerned or the replacement in whole or part of such a surface;

h. Class H: the erection, extension or alteration of an industrial building or a warehouse subject to limitations including on size and location;

i. Class I: certain development carried out on industrial land for the purposes of an industrial process;

j. Class J: development consisting of the provision of a hard surface within the curtilage of an industrial building or warehouse to be used for the purpose of the undertaking concerned or the replacement in whole or part of such a surface;

k. Class K: the deposit of waste material resulting from an industrial process on any land comprised in a site which was used for that purpose on 1st July 1948 whether or not the superficial area or the height of the deposit is extended as a result, but no including material resulting from the winning or working of minerals;

l. Class L: development carried out on land used for the purposes of a waste management facility consisting of: (a) the extension or alteration of a building; and (b) the installation of replacement plant or machinery;

m. Class M: the erection, extension or alteration of a school, college, university or hospital building, subject to limitations including on size and location; and

n. Class N: development consisting of the provision of a hard surface within the curtilage of any school, college, university or hospital to be used for the purposes of that school, college, university or hospital or the replacement in whole or part of such a surface.

CHAPTER TEN

PART 20 – CONSTRUCTION OF NEW DWELLINGHOUSES

145. Part 20 of the GPDO was added in August 2020 with a view to deregulating the planning system and enabling the construction of more houses.

Class ZA: Demolition of buildings and construction of new dwellinghouses in their place

146. Class ZA permits the demolition of certain buildings, including single purpose-built detached blocks of flats and any other single detached building comprising premises established for office use, research and development or certain industrial processes (falling within Classes B1(a), (b) and (c) of the UCO respectively). Those buildings must have existed on 12 March 2020 and they must be replaced with a single building comprising either a purpose-built block of flats or a purpose-build detached dwellinghouse. Class ZA also permits a series of ancillary operations which are listed in para.ZA(3).

147. Paragraph ZA1 includes a long list of exceptions. In particular, this right will not apply if land covered by or within the curtilage of the building to be demolished:

> *(i) is occupied in any part under an agricultural tenancy, unless the express consent of both the landlord and the tenant has been obtained;*
>
> *(ii) is or forms part of article 2(3) land;*
>
> *(iii) is or forms part of a site of special scientific interest;*
>
> *(iv) is or forms part of a listed building or land within its curtilage;*

(v) is or forms part of a scheduled monument or land within its curtilage;

(vi) is or forms part of a safety hazard area;

(vii) is or forms part of a military explosives storage area; or

(viii) is within 3 kilometres of the perimeter of an aerodrome;

148. In addition, a number of criteria apply to the building which is to be demolished, including that it:

a. Must not have been constructed after 31 December 1989;

b. Must not have a footprint in excess of 1,000 square metres;

c. Must not be greater than 18 meters above ground level at any point (not including plant, radio masts and antennae); and

d. Must have been vacant for a period of at least 6 months prior to the date of the application for prior approval.

149. Criteria also apply to the replacement building. These include:

a. The number of storeys in the replacement building must not exceed the number of storeys in the old building by more than two;

b. If the new building has more storeys than the original, the floor to ceiling height of any additional storey, measured internally, must not exceed the greater of the floor to ceiling height of any storey in the old building or 3 metres;

c. The height of the replacement building must not exceed the lower of 7 metres above the height of the old building or 18 meters above ground level.

150. Prior approval is required on a number of matters including design, external appearance, and the impact on the amenity of neighbouring premises.[196]

Class A: New dwellinghouses on detached blocks of flats

151. Class A permits development consisting of works for the construction of up to two additional storeys of flats immediately above the existing topmost residential storey on a building which is a purpose-built, detached block of flats, together specified associated operations.

152. There are some parallels between this right and sch.2, pt.1, Class AA save this right applies to blocks of flats rather than dwellinghouses, and it provides for the creation of new flats rather than the enlargement of a dwellinghouse. It is subject to similar exceptions and conditions. The height of the extended building (not including plant) cannot exceed 30 metres.[197]

Class AA: New dwellinghouses on detached buildings in commercial or mixed use

153. Class AA is similar to Class A save that it permits the erection up to two storeys of dwellinghouses on a building which is:

> *(a) used for any purpose within Class A1 (shops), Class A2 (financial and professional services), Class A3 (restaurants and cafes) or Class B1(a) (offices) of the Schedule to the Use Classes Order, or as a betting office, pay day loan shop or launderette;*

---

[196] GPDO, sch.2, pt.20, para.ZA2.

[197] GPDO, sch,2, pt.20, para.A1(h)

(b) in a mixed use combining—

(i) two or more uses within paragraph (a); or

(ii) a use falling within Class C3 (dwellinghouses) of the Schedule to the Use Classes Order, together with one or more uses within paragraph (a).

154. Similar exceptions and conditions apply to Class A. In particular, Class AA will not apply where the building is less than three storeys in height above ground level. The finished extended building must not be more than 7 metres higher (not including plant) than the existing building. The height of the extended building (not including plant) must not exceed 30 metres.[198]

Class AB: New dwellinghouses on terrace buildings in commercial or mixed use

155. This right is very similar to Class AA save that it applies to terrace buildings and so, accordingly, is subject to greater restrictions, particularly on height which must not exceed 18 metres. In addition, the highest part of the roof of the extended building should not exceed by more than 3.5 metres the height of the highest part of the roof of every other building in the row of terrace buildings of which it forms part (not including plant, in each case).

Class AC: New dwellinghouses on terrace buildings in use as dwellinghouses

156. This right allows for construction of new flats on top of a terrace building in use as a single dwellinghouse. Two storeys may be added where the existing building consists of two or more storeys; one storey may be added where the existing building consists of one storey. Very similar exceptions and conditions apply to those which apply to Class AB. However, it should be noted that, unlike AA and AB, Classes AC and AD (below) do not grant permission for

[198] GPDO, sch,2, pt.20, para.AA1(h)

associated works for the construction of storage, waste or other ancillary facilities reasonably necessary to support the new dwellinghouses. Planning permission would need to be sought for these.

Class AD: New dwellinghouses on detached buildings in use as dwellinghouses

157. This right is similar to Class AC save that it applies to detached dwellinghouses. It is subject to similar exceptions and conditions to Class AC, save it is not limited by the height of other buildings on the terrace.

MORE BOOKS BY LAW BRIEF PUBLISHING

A selection of our other titles available now:-

'A Practical Guide to Solicitor and Client Costs – 2nd Edition' by Robin Dunne
'Constructive Dismissal – Practice Pointers and Principles' by Benjimin Burgher
'A Practical Guide to Religion and Belief Discrimination Claims in the Workplace' by Kashif Ali
'A Practical Guide to the Law of Medical Treatment Decisions' by Ben Troke
'Fundamental Dishonesty and QOCS in Personal Injury Proceedings: Law and Practice' by Jake Rowley
'A Practical Guide to the Law in Relation to School Exclusions' by Charlotte Hadfield & Alice de Coverley
'A Practical Guide to Divorce for the Silver Separators' by Karin Walker
'The Right to be Forgotten – The Law and Practical Issues' by Melissa Stock
'A Practical Guide to Planning Law and Rights of Way in National Parks, the Broads and AONBs' by James Maurici QC, James Neill et al
'A Practical Guide to Election Law' by Tom Tabori
'A Practical Guide to the Law in Relation to Surrogacy' by Andrew Powell
'A Practical Guide to Claims Arising from Fatal Accidents – 2nd Edition' by James Patience
'A Practical Guide to the Ownership of Employee Inventions – From Entitlement to Compensation' by James Tumbridge & Ashley Roughton
'A Practical Guide to Asbestos Claims' by Jonathan Owen & Gareth McAloon
'A Practical Guide to Stamp Duty Land Tax in England and Northern Ireland' by Suzanne O'Hara
'A Practical Guide to the Law of Farming Partnerships' by Philip Whitcomb

'Covid-19, Homeworking and the Law – The Essential Guide to Employment and GDPR Issues' by Forbes Solicitors
'Covid-19, Force Majeure and Frustration of Contracts – The Essential Guide' by Keith Markham
'Covid-19 and Criminal Law – The Essential Guide' by Ramya Nagesh
'Covid-19 and Family Law in England and Wales – The Essential Guide' by Safda Mahmood
'A Practical Guide to the Law of Unlawful Eviction and Harassment – 2nd Edition' by Stephanie Lovegrove
'Covid-19, Residential Property, Equity Release and Enfranchisement – The Essential Guide' by Paul Sams and Louise Uphill
'Covid-19, Brexit and the Law of Commercial Leases – The Essential Guide' by Mark Shelton
'A Practical Guide to Costs in Personal Injury Claims – 2nd Edition' by Matthew Hoe
'A Practical Guide to the General Data Protection Regulation (GDPR) – 2nd Edition' by Keith Markham
'Ellis on Credit Hire – Sixth Edition' by Aidan Ellis & Tim Kevan
'A Practical Guide to Working with Litigants in Person and McKenzie Friends in Family Cases' by Stuart Barlow
'Protecting Unregistered Brands: A Practical Guide to the Law of Passing Off' by Lorna Brazell
'A Practical Guide to Secondary Liability and Joint Enterprise Post-Jogee' by Joanne Cecil & James Mehigan
'A Practical Guide to the Pre-Action RTA Claims Protocol for Personal Injury Lawyers' by Antonia Ford
'A Practical Guide to Neighbour Disputes and the Law' by Alexander Walsh
'A Practical Guide to Forfeiture of Leases' by Mark Shelton
'A Practical Guide to Coercive Control for Legal Practitioners and Victims' by Rachel Horman

‘A Practical Guide to Rights Over Airspace and Subsoil’ by Daniel Gatty
‘Tackling Disclosure in the Criminal Courts – A Practitioner’s Guide’ by Narita Bahra QC & Don Ramble
‘A Practical Guide to the Law of Driverless Cars – Second Edition’ by Alex Glassbrook, Emma Northey & Scarlett Milligan
‘A Practical Guide to TOLATA Claims’ by Greg Williams
‘Artificial Intelligence – The Practical Legal Issues’ by John Buyers
‘A Practical Guide to the Law of Prescription in Scotland’ by Andrew Foyle
‘A Practical Guide to the Construction and Rectification of Wills and Trust Instruments’ by Edward Hewitt
‘A Practical Guide to the Law of Bullying and Harassment in the Workplace’ by Philip Hyland
‘How to Be a Freelance Solicitor: A Practical Guide to the SRA-Regulated Freelance Solicitor Model’ by Paul Bennett
‘A Practical Guide to Prison Injury Claims’ by Malcolm Johnson
‘A Practical Guide to the Small Claims Track’ by Dominic Bright
‘A Practical Guide to Advising Clients at the Police Station’ by Colin Stephen McKeown-Beaumont
‘A Practical Guide to Antisocial Behaviour Injunctions’ by Iain Wightwick
‘Practical Mediation: A Guide for Mediators, Advocates, Advisers, Lawyers, and Students in Civil, Commercial, Business, Property, Workplace, and Employment Cases’ by Jonathan Dingle with John Sephton
‘The Mini-Pupillage Workbook’ by David Boyle
‘A Practical Guide to Crofting Law’ by Brian Inkster
‘A Practical Guide to Spousal Maintenance’ by Liz Cowell
‘A Practical Guide to the Law of Domain Names and Cybersquatting’ by Andrew Clemson
‘A Practical Guide to the Law of Gender Pay Gap Reporting’ by Harini Iyengar

'A Practical Guide to the Rights of Grandparents in Children Proceedings' by Stuart Barlow
'NHS Whistleblowing and the Law' by Joseph England
'Employment Law and the Gig Economy' by Nigel Mackay & Annie Powell
'A Practical Guide to Noise Induced Hearing Loss (NIHL) Claims' by Andrew Mckie, Ian Skeate, Gareth McAloon
'An Introduction to Beauty Negligence Claims – A Practical Guide for the Personal Injury Practitioner' by Greg Almond
'Intercompany Agreements for Transfer Pricing Compliance' by Paul Sutton
'Zen and the Art of Mediation' by Martin Plowman
'A Practical Guide to the SRA Principles, Individual and Law Firm Codes of Conduct 2019 – What Every Law Firm Needs to Know' by Paul Bennett
'A Practical Guide to Adoption for Family Lawyers' by Graham Pegg
'A Practical Guide to Industrial Disease Claims' by Andrew Mckie & Ian Skeate
'A Practical Guide to Redundancy' by Philip Hyland
'A Practical Guide to Vicarious Liability' by Mariel Irvine
'A Practical Guide to Applications for Landlord's Consent and Variation of Leases' by Mark Shelton
'A Practical Guide to Relief from Sanctions Post-Mitchell and Denton' by Peter Causton
'A Practical Guide to Equity Release for Advisors' by Paul Sams
'A Practical Guide to the Law Relating to Food' by Ian Thomas
'A Practical Guide to Financial Services Claims' by Chris Hegarty
'The Law of Houses in Multiple Occupation: A Practical Guide to HMO Proceedings' by Julian Hunt
'A Practical Guide to Unlawful Eviction and Harassment' by Stephanie Lovegrove
'Occupiers, Highways and Defective Premises Claims: A Practical Guide Post-Jackson – 2nd Edition' by Andrew Mckie

www.ingramcontent.com/pod-product-compliance
Lightning Source LLC
LaVergne TN
LVHW022303200926
848481LV00004B/1202
9781913715335